The Mystery of Death and Beyond

Other Books of Interest from St. Augustine's Press

The Mystery of Death and Beyond

Kenneth Baker, S.J.

ST. AUGUSTINE'S PRESS
South Bend, Indiana

Manufactured in the United States of America.

1 2 3 4 5 6   25 24 23 22 21 20 19

Library of Congress Cataloging in Publication Data
Names: Baker, Kenneth, 1929- author.
Title: The mystery of death and beyond / Kenneth Baker, S.J.
Description: 1st [edition].
South Bend, Indiana : St. Augustines Press, 2016.
Includes bibliographical references and index.
Identifiers: LCCN 2016012560
ISBN 9781587315459 (paperbound : alk. paper)
Subjects: LCSH: Death--Religious aspects--Catholic Church.
Future life--Catholic Church.
Death--Religious aspects--Christianity.
Future   life--Christianity.
Classification: LCC BT825 .B263 2016 | DDC 236/.1--dc23 LC
record available at https://lccn.loc.gov/2016012560

∞ The paper used in this publication meets the minimum requirements of the American National Standard for Information Sciences - Permanence of Paper for Printed Materials, ANSI Z39.48-1984.

St. Augustine's Press
www.staugustine.net

Contents

INTRODUCTION

Dear Reader:

I know it is probably difficult for you to pick up this book about death because death is an unpleasant subject for most of us. Normal human beings, busy with their life, work, family and friends, do not like to think about death and prefer to avoid it in conversation, unless perhaps to say that someone they knew "passed away"—carefully avoiding the word "death." In spite of that, you did pick up this book, perhaps out of curiosity, because you know, deep down, that you are going to die and you would like to know what is going to happen to you when you die. Perhaps you are thinking: maybe this book will help me to deal with the problem of death. Young people do not think about death because, for them, it is only a *remote* possibility. They have just begun to live and most of their life is still to come. Old people, however, think a lot about death because most of their life is behind them and they have only a few months or years to live.

We love our life and want to preserve it because it is our greatest possession. Death means the end of life as we know it, separation from family and possessions; it is mysterious to us because what it really means is hidden from us. At death our body is placed in the cold ground and our soul is in the hands of God. Precisely what will happen to my personal existence is not known because no one has ever come back from the grave to tell us what he found on the other side.

In addition to being mysterious death also is accompanied with suffering and helplessness. That is another reason for wanting not to think about it. But the reality of the dying process is most evident to those who work in a hospital and to those who visit a nursing home where old people are dying a slow death. Most of them cannot care for themselves and those who can still move around do so with the help of a walker or a wheelchair. They have lost most of their independence, which we all treasure, and continue to live only because of the care given to them by others.

Thinking about my death is important because how I die, as a friend or enemy of God, will determine my eternal future in the next life—either in heaven with God, the angels and the saints, or in hell with Satan, the devils and the damned. As a Catholic Christian and follower of Jesus Christ I know with complete certitude that my soul is immortal and that I will continue to live on in the next life forever—either in heaven or in hell. There is no other possibility. The thought of heaven and eternal happiness is pleasant. Most Christians, Protestant and Catholic, think that they are going to heaven, even those who do not practice their religion. In America, at the present time, it seems that most people do not believe in the existence of hell or, if they do believe in it, they think that no one is there except the devils. In any event, the thought of hell and eternal punishment, with no end and no escape, is horrifying, so most people do not want to think about it. Most Christians who still believe in hell do not think that it is a real possibility for them. Many use the word "hell" in daily conversation in order to emphasize some point, but they do not reflect on what it really means and they do not think that they could ever end up there.

Another reason for thinking about death is that it is absolutely certain that I will die. In the Letter to the Hebrews we read that "it is appointed for men once to die, and after that comes judgment" (Heb. 9:27). The famous men and women of ancient times and recent history are all dead and buried. So death comes to all, sooner or later; it comes to babies in the womb; it comes to children and teenagers; it comes to mature adults; it comes to all the elderly. Many now live to be a hundred years old because of modern medical science, but shortly after that they die like all those they knew in their youth.

Man is mortal. This means that every human person is in danger of death from the first moment of his conception in the womb of his mother. Millions die every year in the womb and never see the light of day. Millions of young children before the age of five die from disease and malnutrition. Thousands of teenagers die each year from disease, car accidents, drug abuse and suicide. So it is not just those who are over sixty or seventy years of age who are in danger of death. We are all in danger of death during the length of our mortal life on this earth, whether that life is short or long.

Man is mortal. That is part of his nature so he can never change it by his own efforts. Death is like a shadow that follows us wherever we go. Many of the things we do every day are designed to prevent death. To stay alive we have to breathe fresh air, eat healthy food, drink liquids, sleep, cleanse the body, relieve nature, avoid falling down when we walk, be careful crossing a busy street, be an alert and safe driver of a car, and so forth.

We are all susceptible of sickness and disease. We get sick with a cold, not knowing how we contracted it. We eat something in a restaurant that makes us sick. If we shake hands with someone with a contagious disease, we come down with the same disease. All of these maladies are related to death in some way, because they are effects of our mortality. Most of us die slowly—not noticeable in youth but very obvious in a hospital or nursing home for the elderly. Soldiers on the battlefield die suddenly. People in serious car accidents and airplane accidents die suddenly. Old people die suddenly from a heart attack or a stroke.

The point I am making here is that our whole life, constantly and wherever we are, is under the threat of death. Most people, especially the young, do not seem to be aware of this. Older people tend to be more aware of impending death because most of their life is behind them and each day they are one day closer to dying; also, their relatives and friends have either died or have serious health problems.

The mortality of man is absolute and unavoidable. Every human being from Adam until now, perhaps with the exception of Elijah and Henoch in the Old Testament, has died. Every human being alive today on earth will die eventually. This will continue to be the case until the Second Coming of Christ and the end of the world, when God will make all things new, as St. John tells us in the Book of Revelation (Rev. 21:5).

We can never be sure about living in the future, because the future is unknown to us and unknowable. Since man is mortal, at any moment he can die from many different causes. You do not have absolute certitude that you will be alive tomorrow—or next week. *The Imitation of Christ* (Book I, ch. 23) says that in the morning you should imagine that you will not live till night; "and when evening comes presume not to promise yourself the next morning." The purpose of this is always to be prepared and to live in such a manner that death may never find you unprepared to meet Christ who will judge you and determine your destiny for all eternity.

God became man in Jesus Christ, who assumed our human nature. He came into this world to die for us so that we can receive forgiveness of our sins and life everlasting. It was his painful *death* on the Cross that accomplished our redemption. Because of Christ, those who believe in him and are baptized possess the grace of life of God so that when they die they will go to heaven and be happy forever—something we all desire. The death of Christ means life for us.

We were created for eternity, but now we live in time. Each minute, each hour, each day, each event has a beginning and an end. Since our life is in time, we have a beginning and an end. In heaven (and in hell) there is a beginning but no end—they are both a perpetual now.

The Christian answer to the mystery of death and beyond, and to the fear of death, is faith in Jesus Christ and acceptance of what the Catholic Church teaches about the divinity of Christ and the reality of the Holy Trinity. Through faith in Christ and in his Church, of which he is the Head, we know that death is the door, the gate, the entrance into eternal life. In her Liturgy the Church often reminds us to prefer heavenly and eternal things to the material and temporal things of this earth.

The wise person prepares for death beginning in his youth. He prepares himself by obeying God and by living a virtuous life of love of God and neighbor. God is love—that is his definition. He has destined each one of us to be united to him in love for all eternity. So the goal and purpose of human life is to grow in love—love of God and love of neighbor. Those who do that are fulfilling the purpose that God had in creating them and they are preparing themselves for a death that will result in everlasting life. We all seek life and try to hold on to it for as long as we can; God who created each one of us is infinite life. This means that our desire for life can be fulfilled only through union with God who is life by his very nature.

Dear Reader, the purpose of this book is to help you to think clearly about your death. It is to urge you to give serious thought to the fact that your life on planet earth will be short and that it is a preparation for a better, glorious life in heaven that will go on forever with no possibility of losing it. These thoughts on death have been assembled to motivate you to live in such a way that, when the day and hour of your death comes to you, you will die a Happy Death, that is, in the state of sanctifying grace because you spent your life striving to do the will of God for you and because you have accepted in faith and love in advance the death that God has planned for you.

Kenneth Baker, S.J.

CHAPTER 1: THE FACT OF DEATH

You are dust, and to dust you shall return. (Gen. 3:19)

"Remember, man, that you are dust to dust you shall return." With these solemn words taken from Genesis 3:19 the priest on Ash Wednesday makes the Sign of the Cross with ashes on our forehead to remind us that we are frail, fragile human beings, that our life is like the dust that is here today and gone tomorrow, that we were created by God from the dust of the earth and that we are destined to return there when we die—either sooner or later. Each year many Catholics who receive the ashes on the first day of Lent, receive them for the last time since they die in the course of the year. The ashes also remind us of the words in the Book of Ecclesiastes, "Vanity of vanities and all is vanity" (12:8). *The Imitation of Christ* expands this by adding the words "except to love God and serve him alone" (Bk. I, 1).

Life is a gift from God who is subsistent life and the source of all life. Everything living strives to preserve itself in being. Man, because he has a mind and will open to all being, deep down wants to live forever but he is threatened with death every day from the moment of his conception in the womb of his mother. Man, like all other living material beings, is composed of parts which in time are separated; when that happens he dies and his body is buried in the ground. There is no escape so death comes to all. Death can come slowly, as it does to those dying in a nursing home; it can come quickly in an automobile accident or from a heart attack or a stroke. Death follows man like his shadow on a sunny day—there is no escape. Nevertheless, man instinctively feels that there is something wrong about death, that it should not be, that he should not have to die. Death means the end and dissolution of man's personal existence that he has known since childhood and he does not know what will happen to him after death; death is mysterious.

Perhaps that is the reason why most men and women fear death and will do almost anything to avoid or delay it.

Young people often do not come in contact with death unless it is the death of a grandparent whom they perhaps do not know very well. Once a person lives to be sixty and beyond, the death of relatives and friends happens with increased regularity. A relative who is my age remarked a few years ago when a classmate died: "I used to go to weddings all the time; now all I do is go to wakes and funerals."

One thing about death that impresses me is that it is universal—no one escapes it. No matter how powerful and how famous a person may be—a pope, a president, an author of many books, a movie star, a scientist—they all die eventually. I like to watch old films made before 1960. The thought often comes to me that all these actors, once famous and rich, are now dead—John Wayne, Bette Davis, Clark Gable, Cary Grant, Grace Kelly, Bob Hope, Bing Crosby, Frank Sinatra, Elizabeth Taylor and scores of others. Where are they now? Each one was created by God for himself—that they might attain heaven and the Beatific Vision. I hope they all made it since that is the ultimate purpose of human existence on this earth of time and space. Each person is given a certain amount of time to work out his salvation "with fear and trembling" as St. Paul said (Phil. 2:12).

Man is by nature mortal and therefore he is always in danger of death from the first moment of his conception in his mother's womb until the moment of his death. It seems to me that many of the things we do every day we do to delay death as long as possible. Good health is very precious because is guarantees the continuance of life. Bad health is to be avoided at all costs because it is a signal of approaching death. In order to promote good health and so to protect ourselves from death we need sufficient food, drink, sleep, clothing and shelter. Americans are addicted to taking billions of pills every day to cure various ailments and to prevent sickness which leads to death.

The danger of death is all around us and we are reminded of it many times every day, at least implicitly. The medical and pharmaceutical businesses are huge because they promise good health and avoidance or delay of death. The new environmental campaign has to do with good air and good water so that people will be healthy and not in danger of death. Death is a major preoccupation of our literature since murder mysteries are a popular form of entertainment in such authors as Agatha Christie and Mary Higgins Clark. War stories and war films, like "Saving Private Ryan," are a popular form of entertainment. Murder, death and dying are major themes in the electronic media. The point I want to make here is that we are constantly in danger of death, even though we do not think about it explicitly. Every day in America thousands of people die not only from sickness and old age, but also in car accidents, so we are all in danger of death every time we drive or ride in an automobile.

Man is also by nature religious. Some form of religion is found among all peoples of all time. There is an intimate connection between religion and death because worship of God or the gods is related to warding off evil and seeking favorable treatment in the next world after death, however it is thought of.

Man is by nature mortal, but his first parents, Adam and Eve, were created immortal by God, as we read in Genesis 2 and 3. God endowed them in Paradise with the preternatural gift of bodily immortality. In their original state, therefore, they were exempted from the law of death that governs all living material beings. As a punishment for their disobedience, however, they were made subject to the death that God had warned them about. For God had said to them: "Of the tree of the knowledge of good and evil you shall not eat, for in the day that you eat of it you shall die" (Gen. 2:17). That they would suffer and die is made clear in the next chapter: "In the sweat of your face you shall eat bread till you return to the ground, for out of it you were taken; you are dust, and to dust you shall return" (Gen. 3:19).

St. Paul teaches us that death is the consequence of Adam's sin. "As sin came into the world through one man and death through sin, so death spread to all men, because all men sinned" (Rom. 5:12). On this point the Council of Trent said that death is a punishment for sin.[1] But for those who die in the state of

---

1   Denzinger-Hünermann, *Enchiridion Symbolorum* (43rd edition) 1511. In future references Denzinger will be abbreviated as D.

sanctifying grace death is not so much a punishment as it is a consequence of sin. Since Jesus and his Blessed Mother were free from original sin and all personal sin, death for them was not a result of sin; it was rather a consequence of life in a material body.

According to Genesis, St. Paul and the Council of Trent, all human beings, as descendants of Adam and Eve, are subject to original sin (except Jesus and Mary); therefore they are all subject to the law of death. The key biblical text for this point is Romans 5:12ff. St. Paul also says in Hebrews 9:27, "It is appointed for men to die once, and after that comes judgment."

God did not bring about the death of human beings—Adam did by his sin. God created man originally immortal. The Book of Wisdom says that "God did not make death, and he does not delight in the death of the living" (Wis. 1:13). Further on, the sacred author says that "God created man for incorruption…but through the devil's envy death entered the world" (Wis. 2:23-24). So death entered into the world because our first parents, following the suggestion of Satan, violated the express will of God, even after he had warned them that they would die the death if they ate the forbidden fruit.

The reality of death for all human beings is absolutely certain; it is as certain as the first principles of metaphysics. However, the time of death is uncertain. We all know that we will die, even though we do not like to think about it, but we do not know when it will happen. It is a blessing from God that we do not know when we will die. If we did know, it would change our whole approach to daily life. Man is here today and gone tomorrow and few people think about those who have died or pray for them. There is an old saying that two things in life are certain—death and taxes. Some clever individuals may be able to escape taxes, but no one can escape death.

People do not like to talk about death because they do not want to be reminded that they also will soon die. When a relative or friend dies, they often use euphemisms or circumlocutions by saying that he "passed away" or "left us" or "kicked the bucket" in order to avoid using the word "death." There seems to be a growing tendency in our culture to avoid words like "death" and "dying." Every day the media report on killings and people dying in all parts of the world, but they do not offer any analysis on the meaning of death. For most people, especially those without faith in Jesus Christ, the subject is too painful. I read somewhere that a reason why many people like to attend huge sporting events like professional football games is so that they can forget about the reality of impending death.

All human beings fear death and try to avoid it any way they can. This is very natural because existence or life is good and everything strives to preserve itself in being. Elderly men and women spend much of their time and money trying to delay the inevitability of death. They fear the suffering involved in death, but they fear even more what will happen to them after they have died, especially when they think about their past sins. How will God judge them? Will they die in the state of sanctifying grace? Will they go to heaven or to hell? And what about the prospect of suffering in purgatory for those who are saved but still must make satisfaction for the sins they have committed? Because death means entering into a new type of life that is unknown and mysterious, man fears it and tries to delay it as long as possible.

The simplest definition of death on the physical level is that it is the separation of the soul, the principle of life, from the body of a living being. Although we do not know exactly when the soul leaves the body, there are certain signs of death: cessation of breathing and movement of the limbs; coldness to the touch and, after some time, decomposition during which the body falls apart. It returns to the dust from which it was taken.

Corruption of the body is a result of death because the soul, the principle of life and unity, is no longer present. But what happens to the soul? Does the soul perish with the body, or does it live on in a new stage of life without the body? How are we to imagine this? What happens to my personal existence and my consciousness of who I am as a person? As Catholics we know that the soul is spiritual and therefore immortal, that it lives on after it is separated from the body. But what that spiritual life is like we do not know; it is impossible for us to imagine a life without our body—without eyes and ears and mouth and the sense of touch. In the Gospels Jesus speaks about heaven and hell as the permanent dwelling place for those who are saved and for those who are condemned. That is made clear in the parable of the rich man and Lazarus in Luke 16:19-31. Most people, except perhaps some hardened atheists, are very concerned about what will happen to them after they die. But atheists die too and it has often been said during a time of war that "there are no atheists in foxholes."

Because of divine revelation and the infallible teaching of the Church founded by Jesus, Catholics who know their Catechism know more about the next life than many others do. Catholics know that after death those who are saved go either directly to heaven or to purgatory for a time if they need to make satisfaction for the temporal punishment due to sins; those who die in the state of mortal sin go directly to hell. So there are really only two final, permanent possibilities for immortal human souls—heaven or hell. Implied in these two possibilities is the fact that they will be judged by God on the basis of their good and bad deeds while on earth, as St. Paul says in Hebrews 9:27 quoted above. The Catholic Church refers to the judgment immediately after death as the "Particular Judgment" which concerns each individual; this is to be distinguished from the "General Judgment" of all mankind at the end of the world when Christ will come again in glory to judge the living and the dead. This judgment is final and irrevocable. Since God's knowledge is infinite, he knows everything that has ever happened in the world and everything that will happen in the future—including secret thoughts and desires—he knows perfectly the state of soul of each person. Nothing is hidden from his eyes. God knows instantly whether the person is deserving of heaven or hell. There is no need for lawyers and there is no appeal to a higher court. The judgment of each one of us by Jesus after our death is the Supreme Court of heaven from which there is no appeal. We know that his judgment will be true and fair because he is infinitely just and infinitely good.

Most people who live to be forty or older often think about death and what it means. A famous psychiatrist once said that all of his patients over the age of 35 were concerned about the problem of death. Death means the end of man's earthly existence in time and space; it means permanent separation from family and friends. His soul, now separated from his body, enters into eternity—there is no more time for him or her. The time of pilgrimage, trial, suffering, toil and merit is over. He has entered into eternity in which there is no past, present and future such as we experience in time. Eternity is defined as the complete possession of life all at once—it is a perpetual now. Death is also irrevocable. There is no such thing as reincarnation or transmigration of souls as the pantheistic religions teach. Again, as St. Paul says, it is appointed to men once to die, and after this the judgment. There is no second or third chance to determine one's eternal destiny. The blessed who go to heaven will be happy there forever and cannot lose it by sinning or by annihilation; the damned who go to hell will be there forever and cannot escape, either by conversion of heart or by annihilation. Anyone who reflects on the meaning of hell as a place and condition of punishment and suffering that will continue forever, without any rest and without any way of escape, will shudder in horror and will make every effort to live a life of virtue in obedience to God so that his eternal future will be happiness in heaven.

The consideration of these truths brings home to us that death is a serious matter. It is much more serious than the way it is treated in our culture and in our media of news and entertainment. In this changeable life, if one makes a mistake he can correct it and start over again. That does not apply to those who die. You die only one—there is no second chance. The wise person is the one who considers the possibilities and carefully provides for his future.

That being the case, it is extremely important—eternally important—to prepare ourselves for death and not to be caught off guard, because death can come suddenly at any time. Think of those who died instantly in the Twin Towers in New York City on September 11, 2001—those in the airplanes and those in the buildings. The main way of preparing ourselves for death is to lead a life of virtue, to obey God's Ten Commandments, to strive to do God's will at all times. This can be summed up in Jesus' basic command to love God and one's neighbor. In order to remain faithful and to overcome evil temptations which all are subject to, it is essential to pray daily, to practice some self-denial and to be generous to those in need. Also, it is spiritually helpful to think often about death, which will surely come one day. Saints have said that one should live each day as though it were his last day. In the New Testament we read that the Lord will come like a thief in the night—at a time when you do not expect him.[2]

Now is the time to lay up treasures of merit in heaven by receiving the Sacraments regularly, by performing good deeds and by avoiding all sin, both mortal and deliberate venial sin. God made us without asking our consent, but he will not admit us to his beatifying presence without our willing it and working for it. He made us free and he will not violate that freedom, even to save us from hell. We are free to choose either good or evil, so we should work out our salvation in fear and trembling, as St. Paul says in Philippians 2:12. The author of *The Imitation of Christ* says to each one of us: "Be always prepared and live in such a manner that death may never find thee unprovided."[3]

The prayers of the Church over the dead body in her funeral service, prayers that will be said over our dead body when it is brought into the church for the Requiem Mass, stress begging for God's mercy and forgiveness for the dead person and granting him or her the gift of eternal life in heaven. The prayers presuppose the reality and certainty of eternal life—in heaven with Christ for those who die in the state of sanctifying grace, and in hell for those who die unrepentant in the state of mortal sin as enemies of God. With the Church we beseech God: "Eternal rest grant unto him, O Lord, and let perpetual light shine upon him. May his soul, and the souls of all the faithful departed, through the mercy of God, rest in peace. Amen."

Because of his death and resurrection, Jesus merited eternal life for all those who share in his life through faith, love and divine grace which is the supernatural life of the soul. Because he accepted our death in an act of free submission to the will of his Father, Jesus' obedience has transformed the curse of death into

2   Rev. 3:3. See also 1 Thess. 5:2, 4; 2 Pet. 3:10; Rev. 16:15. Profound thoughts about death are presented in *The Imitation of Christ*, Book I, Chapter 23.
3   Book I, 23, 3.

a blessing.[4] Thus, because of the death of Jesus on the cross the death of the Christian has a positive meaning. As St. Paul said, "The saying is sure: if we have died with him, we will also live with him" (2 Tim. 2:11). For the Christian believer, therefore, death is entrance into eternal life with Christ.

We Catholics are a people of hope because we live spiritually by the life of Christ. So for us death is not the end of life; it is the beginning of eternal life that no one can take away from us. St. Thérèse of Lisieux on her death bed said: "I am not dying, I am entering life."[5]

Because Christians in the state of sanctifying grace die "in Christ" the Church prays in the Preface of Christian Death (Roman Missal): "Lord, for your faithful people life is changed, not ended. When the body of our earthly dwelling lies in death, we gain an everlasting place in heaven."

In the beginning God created man immortal. By his sin and the misuse of freedom, Adam rebelled against God and so brought death into the world for himself and all his descendants. God positively willed that man should not die, but there was one condition—that he should not eat of the tree of the knowledge of good and evil. Since God made man free, for his own mysterious reasons he permitted Adam to misuse his freedom, to sin and so to incur the punishment of death for himself and for all of his descendants. But in his providence he decreed that what we lost in Adam we should recover superabundantly through the Incarnation, life, death and resurrection of Jesus Christ, the only Son of God and the Savior of all mankind. It was the will of God that what we lost in Adam we should regain in Christ, the Second Adam. This is a striking example of the infinite power and providence of God who can bring good out of evil.

The fact of death is a serious problem for the human person. Man instinctively feels that there is something wrong about death. Our knowledge of death comes from observation and daily experience. But we do not have any "inside" knowledge

4   *Catechism of the Catholic Church* 1009. Henceforth it will be shortened to CCC.
5   CCC 1011, note 582.

of death because no one has ever died and then come back to explain to us the nature and meaning of this experience. When we reflect on the meaning of death two apparently contradictory aspects of it come to mind. On the one hand, death seems to be quite natural since all living things like plants and animals go through the same cycle of birth, growth, maturity, and then death and dissolution. Since man has a living body like other animals, death for him seems to be the natural conclusion of his life. On the other hand, death seems to be absurd and to conflict with his desire to go on living forever. Is death really natural for man? Or is it really unnatural because of the spiritual and immaterial nature of the human soul? If it were natural, man would not sense that there is something wrong with death, something absurd.

St. Thomas Aquinas said that death and other defects connected with it are not natural to man. Perhaps this is the reason why we fear it and resist it. His reason for saying that is based on the spirituality and the immortality of the human soul. He is thinking here of the original state of Adam and Eve who were created in grace and given the preternatural gift of immortality because their purpose of existence was to attain the Beatific Vision of God in heaven for all eternity. Because man has a rational, spiritual soul and has a supernatural end or purpose in life, the relation of his soul to his body is different from that of all other animals. When they die, everything returns to the potency of matter, nothing survives—there is no dog or cat heaven; when a human person dies, the soul lives on but the body returns to the dust from which it was taken by the creative power of God.

St. Thomas offers three arguments for his position that death is not natural for man. First, he says that God made in man everything that is natural in him. But we know from divine revelation in the Bible that God did not make death (Wis. 1:13). Therefore he concludes that death is not natural to man.

The second argument goes like this: what is natural to any being cannot be called a punishment or an evil, since what is natural to anything is suitable to it. But death is a punishment for original sin, as St. Paul says in Romans 5:12. Therefore death is not natural to man.

The third argument is a bit more difficult. He says that matter is proportionate to its form and everything is proportionate to its end or purpose. Man's end is everlasting happiness and the form of the human body is the rational soul. Therefore the human body is naturally incorruptible.[6]

If that is so, then why do all men and women die? The answer is the original sin of Adam. God warned him that he would die if he ate of the fruit of the forbidden tree. He and Eve sinned and this was followed with the punishment of suffering and death for them and all their descendants. Since we are all descendants of Adam and Eve, we share in their punishment and so we have to die.

Man is not like anything else on this planet earth because he is the only living being that has a rational soul. Man can think; he can reason and he can make free choices. He has self-consciousness and self-reflection; this means that he not only knows things outside of himself, but also that he knows that he knows. He can reflect back on his own acts; no material body can do that. Man has self-reflection because his mind is not material—it is a spiritual reality that transcends time and space and is not the function of a bodily organ.

The absurdity of death in the life of the human person comes to light in the universal fear of death. Because man can reflect back on himself, because he can make free choices and is aware of his own personal existence, because he can think about what will or might happen to him in the future, death is seen as a threat to his personal existence. Man wants to remain in possession of himself and to assert his freedom, but death, which is contrary to his will, seems to mean the loss of freedom and everything else.

Because man's mind is spiritual and open to all reality, he transcends the present time and so can think about the future which he does not know. Cows, dogs, cats and all brute animals cannot do that because they are totally material and bound to the here and now. Cows and pigs do not worry about their future in the slaughter house because they know nothing about the future and what will happen to them.

6   St. Thomas Aquinas, *Summa Theologiae* I-II, 85, 6. Henceforth the *Summa* will be shortened to STh.

The knowledge from philosophy and revelation that the human soul is immortal, and that it will continue to exist after death, does not overcome man's fearful apprehension in the face of death. All of our experiences up to the time of death have been in the body and all of our knowledge has come to us through our senses. Separation of the soul from the body seems strange to us. Based on all previous experience it is an unnatural situation. The thought of living and acting without a body—without eyes, ears and limbs—seems strange and unnatural to us. All of this contributes to our fear of dying.

The two basic attitudes towards death that are most common are that of the materialist or atheist and that of the Christian believer. The atheist can see no overall purpose to the universe, except what he can devise with the help of Darwinian evolution which has been called "the engine of atheism." Evolution helps him explain the obvious presence of purpose or finality in the world without the help of a Supreme Intelligence or God. But his own personal existence, for him, has no purpose and so is absurd. For such atheists the logical way to exit this life when they get old or sick or despondent is to commit suicide. Their denial of God implies also the denial of the immortality of the soul. For them everything is material and temporal; for them there is no such thing as an immortal soul and eternal life.

That is what they say and write about, especially when they are young and healthy and death is remote. But since man's soul is by nature immortal, and since each man is made for God and eternal life, I suspect that for them there is always a lurking fear and suspicion, which they refuse to admit explicitly, that they might be wrong, especially when they see that they are surrounded with people who believe in life after death.

The second possible attitude towards death is that of the Christian and religious person. The Christian accepts the problem of death and the afterlife as an indication of his lack of knowledge about how he fits into the totality of reality. He recognizes that he does not have comprehensive knowledge about his own existence. This prepares him to be willing to accept from divine revelation the solution of the problem of death—a solution that will satisfy his curiosity about the full meaning of life and death. Since God created man and made him immortal with a supernatural destiny, only he can give man an insight into what awaits him in the next life after the experience of death. St. Paul was given a glimpse of what awaits man in the next life, but it exceeds even his power of expression, as he says in 1 Cor. 2:9, "Eye has not seen, nor ear heard, nor the human heart conceived, what God has prepared for those who love him." And concerning his own mystical experience he said that he was "caught up into Paradise and heard things that are not to be told, that no mortal is permitted to repeat" (2 Cor. 12:4). A mystery is something we know about but do not fully comprehend. There are natural mysteries like life and death, and there are supernatural mysteries revealed to us by God, such as the Holy Trinity and the Incarnation of the Word of God in Jesus Christ. In the next chapter we will consider what we can know about the mystery of death from the Bible and what we do not know.

CHAPTER 2: DEATH IN THE BIBLE

*God did not make death, and he does not delight
in the death of the living. (Wis. 1:13)*

Death in the Old Testament

The sad fact of death for all mankind is mentioned often in the
Old Testament (OT) and it is regularly associated with man's
creatureliness: man was made by God from the dust of the earth
and he is destined to return to dust (Gen. 2:7; 3:19; Ps. 90:3; Job
34:15; Eccles. 12:7). Man has to go "the way of all the earth"
(Josh. 23:14; 1 Kings 2:2) and he will fade away like the flowers
of the field (Ps. 103:15). The authors complain about death as
the end of life, but they accept it from God as something unavoidable (Job 7:7–11). Life is considered as a supremely good
gift from God and one is very reluctant to give it up unless it is
absolutely necessary (Job 2:4; Eccles. 9:4; Sir. 41:2). Still, the
pious Hebrew in the OT accepted both life and death from God
as the absolute ruler of the world (1 Sam. 2:6; Ps. 90:10) and a
long life with many children and grandchildren is looked upon
as a special grace and gift of God (Gen. 25:8; Job 42:17).

A long life and avoidance of death as long as possible in the
OT was considered to be very desirable. The thinking we find
in the Pentateuch is that a long life is the reward from God for
obedience to the covenant with the Lord (see Deut. 5:16; 16:20).
Much thinking about death and what lies beyond is found in
the wisdom literature of the OT. In that framework, wisdom is
good and leads to a long life, while foolishness or sin leads to
death.

In the apocalyptic passages of the OT there are a few hints
of hope for some kind of survival after death (Isa. 25:8; Dan.
12:2). But a big problem for them was the death of the young,

the death of the innocent and the sudden death of an adult (Ps. 102:23–24; Jer. 17:11). Thus, an early or sudden death is considered a disaster or a consequence of the wrath of God (Job 22:16; Jer. 17:11). In the early parts of the Bible, especially in the Pentateuch, the problem of early or sudden death is reflected on and is also linked with sin. Genesis spells out in graphic details that man is subject to trials, suffering and death because he has separated himself from God by his sin. The shortening of man's life to 120 years is seen as a punishment from God (Gen. 6:3). And the punishment meted out to Eve of pain in childbirth and to Adam of toil and sweat is contained in God's threat and warning after their sin (see Gen. 3:16–19). The result of his threat is that their life will be full of bitterness and disappointment; they will live for a short time and then they will have to die the death.

It should be noted here that the word "death" in the OT has a broad meaning and includes more than just dying. It is also related to evil and to the tribulations of daily life. The idea that death is the result of sin appears in Sirach 25:24: "From a woman sin had its beginning, and because of her we all die." The book of Wisdom repeats this idea and attributes it to the devil: "[B]ut through the devil's envy death entered the world" (2:23).

The future that awaits man in sheol, the underworld, is very bleak. In the thinking of the Psalmist the dead seem to have no existence: "Look away from me, that I may know gladness, before I depart and be no more" (Ps. 39:13). But the thinking of the ancients was that something of man persists after death. The body may be in the grave, but something of the dead person continues to exist in sheol. What that is they do not know, but it is described in terms of shadows, a gaping hole, a deep pit and a place of silence and darkness (Ps. 115:17; 88:12ff.). God forgets the dead and once they have passed through the gates of sheol there is no return (Ps. 88:6). This idea is stated clearly in Job 21:20–22: "Are not the days of my life few? Let me alone, that I may find a little comfort before I go whence I shall not return, to the land of gloom and deep darkness, the land of gloom and chaos, where light is as darkness." In the OT this is what man has to look forward to when he dies.

In the thinking of the Israelites dead bodies are "unclean" and so is the grave where they are placed. Also, living persons who touch the bodies of the dead were considered unclean and they have to be purified before they can associate with others. This idea of "unclean," however, protected the pious people of the OT from having anything to do with consulting the dead and getting involved in necromancy, which was common among the neighboring pagan peoples and also among the Greeks. King Saul banned the mediums and wizards from Israel, and then he went against his own law when he consulted the woman medium at Endor because he wanted to consult with the dead prophet, Samuel (1 Sam. 28:3ff.).

A study of the texts in the OT about death reveals that the true believers in the Lord God of Israel did not have a very positive idea about death and the afterlife. In the last books of the OT—those written during the 200 years before Christ, such as Wisdom and 1 and 2 Maccabees—we find explicit reference to the immortality of the soul, but no clarity about the nature of that life after death. The clear and full revelation about life after death was not made known to us until the preaching of the Gospel by Jesus Christ, the only Son of God, the Image of the heavenly Father and, after his glorious resurrection, the One who sends us the Holy Spirit. Jesus sees the Father, is one with the Father (John 14:9); he is the source of life and is the one who conquered death: "I am the way, and the truth, and the life" (John 4:6). Jesus is the only one who has the "words of everlasting life" (John 6:68; 17:3).[1]

Death in the New Testament

The reality of death and its close connection with sin is a major theme in the New Testament (NT). The word "death" appears in some context on almost every page of the NT. Death is seen as the power of evil and a result of the power of the devil over

---

[1] The following sources were used in preparing this section: *Lexikon für Theologie und Kirche* (1965; LThK) 10, "Tod," 218–219; X. Leon-Dufour, *Dictionary of Biblical Theology* (Desclee 1967), "Death," 93–95.

this world. Human history appears as a drama of life and death until the coming of Jesus Christ. By his death and resurrection he triumphs over death. Now those who have faith in him and are baptized share in his victory over death and have become a new humanity with an eternal destiny in heaven. Jesus is the light shining on those who sit in the shadow of death (see Matt. 4:16; Luke 1:79). In the thinking of the synoptic gospels this "light" is manifested and obvious when Jesus raised the dead to life, as in the case of Lazarus (see Matt. 11:5).

There is no clear "theology" of death in the synoptic gospels, but there is such a theology in the letters of St. Paul.[2] The reason for this is that Paul is thinking mainly about the two major events in the life of Christ and in the Christian preaching—his death and resurrection. For Paul Christ, as the risen and glorified Lord, is the victor over death (Rom. 5 & 6; 1 Cor. 15). The reality of death, the reason for it and its consequences, runs through the thinking or theology of St. Paul. The author quoted above says that it is the "key" to the theology of St. Paul. Essential parts of Pauline theology are linked to his concept of death: he relates death to his teaching about sin, about the flesh, about the law, about Baptism and about moral conduct. Paul sees man's existence on this earth of time and space as an area of tension between life and death and he interprets the meaning of the Christ event above all from the reality of his death and resurrection.

First of all, death entered the world because of the sin of Adam (Rom. 5:12; 6:23; 7:13; Eph. 2:1). The worldwide power of sin is clearly seen in the corruption of death which awaits each person (Rom. 5:14, 17, 21). The law of the OT was not able to free man from death, but God did it by sending his Son in the likeness of the flesh subject to sin. Through the Spirit of life working in him he has set us free from the law of sin and death (Rom. 8:2f.). Because of sin our body is still under the power of physical death, but the corruption of death of the faithful Christian is already basically overcome through the Holy Spirit of Christ that dwells in him through faith and Baptism. Paul develops this idea in his teaching on Baptism which for him is

2   LThK 10, 220.

something like a death experience. Paul relates Baptism to the death and resurrection of Jesus because the baptized person has been raised to a new and spiritual level of life by sharing the life of Christ who died and rose from the dead (Rom. 6; Col. 2:12; Eph 2:5ff.).

For the Apostle there are also moral consequences for the Christian who is reborn in Christ to a new life. Those who have died and risen with Christ must consider themselves dead to sin but alive to God in Christ Jesus (Rom. 6:–7:7; 8:4–12; Gal. 5:14). When the faithful share in the death of Christ they change and relativize the disaster of earthly death because it is the door or entrance to the still hidden life of glory that will be revealed in the Second Coming of Christ at the end of the world. This truth can give rise to the desire for an early death as a way of escaping the tribulations of daily life on this planet (2 Cor. 5:1–8; Phil. 1:21ff.). According to St. Paul, the coming glory of the resurrected body will prove to be the final victory over the power of death (1 Cor. 15:54ff.).

In the writings of St. John death is seen as a power of this world that is set over against the life of the spirit that Jesus brings into the world. The person who has faith in Jesus Christ now has already "passed from death to life" (John 5:24; 1 John 3:14). The Book of Revelation mentions a "second death" which is eternal damnation (Rev. 20:6, 14; 21:8.). Finally, Death and Hades will be cast into "the lake of fire" after they have been forced to render up the dead to resurrection (Rev. 20:13).

As a result of the death and resurrection of Jesus, and his triumph over Satan and death, bodily death for the Christian takes on a new meaning. It is no longer a disaster one must accept as the result of his sins. The Christian dies with hope in the Lord just as he lived in him (Rom. 14:7f.). From a physical necessity death has become an object of beatitude: "Blessed are they who die in the Lord henceforth. Blessed indeed, says the Spirit, that they may rest from their labors" (Rev. 14:13).

The hope for immortality and resurrection which began to appear in the OT in the two centuries before the coming of Christ becomes a reality in the mystery of Jesus Christ. Our union with his death, through faith and the sacraments, has not only given us a new life, but it has also given us assurance that

"He who raised Christ Jesus from the dead will give life to your mortal bodies through his Spirit who dwells in you" (Rom. 8:11). For the faithful Catholic death is not the end of life; it is a change from this temporal existence to eternal life with God. This truth is beautifully expressed in the Preface for the Mass of Christian Burial: "Lord, for your faithful people life is changed, not ended. When the body of our earthly dwelling lies in death we gain an everlasting dwelling place in heaven."[3]

---

3   Leon-Dufour, *op. cit.*, 95–98; LThK 10, 219–221.

CHAPTER 3:
THE MYSTERY OF DEATH

The wages of sin is death, but the free gift of God is eternal life in
Christ Jesus our Lord. (Rom. 6:23)

The death of a human person is not just an unavoidable evil—
it is also a deep mystery. A mystery is some fact that is veiled or
hidden from us—we know that it exists but we do not fully understand it; we do not comprehend it. From a philosophical
analysis of human thinking and willing, man can come to know
that the human soul is spiritual and therefore immortal. If the
soul is immortal, this means that it continues to live in a new
state, without the body, after the experience of physical death
and separation from the body. But since no human person has
ever come back from the dead to tell us what the next life is like,
we do not know what awaits us when we die.

Another source of knowledge about the next life is from divine revelation. Because of the revelation of Jesus in the New
Testament we do have some knowledge about existence after
death. We know, for example, from the Bible and the teaching
of the Church about the existence of heaven for the saved, hell
for the damned, and purgatory for those who must be purified
before they can enter into heaven and the face to face vision of
the all-holy God. We know that we will all be judged on the
basis of our love and our thoughts, words and deeds during our
earthly life.

All men have to die; in that sense death is a natural phenomenon. The necessity of death destroys man's sense of self-
sufficiency; it makes him realize that he is a creature—that he is
essentially different from God and that he is totally dependent
on God. Man, as a spirit in matter, is mortal and God, who is
infinite in all perfections, is the living source of all life. Man has

his life from God as a free gift—God does not owe man anything, especially the gift of life. Thus, what God gives belongs to him. What he freely gives he can take back, and that is what he does in allowing man to die. This is an indication of the fact that man's ultimate destiny as a human person is not in his own hands but in God's. The full picture, the whole purpose of the earth and the universe is that man may attain eternal life with God as his final destiny and in so doing glorify God.

God's control of the world has special meaning with regard to the survival of the human soul after death. Even though we know that the soul is immortal, we do not know what its activity will be like after separation from the body. In this matter we have to put our trust in the good God who knows everything and who created the human soul to live forever in happiness. Our faith in Jesus Christ, who rose from the dead and is gloriously seated at the right hand of the Father, assures us that we will be well taken care of if we persevere in the grace of God.

In our present temporal situation, however, our concern about death as something to be feared, as a problem, as a seeming absurdity has a solid basis in reality. For we read in the Book of Wisdom: "God did not make death, and he does not delight in the death of the living….God created us for incorruption, and made us in the image of his own eternity, but through the devil's envy death entered the world" (Wis. 1:13; 2:23–24). Death, therefore, is a consequence of sin—through the original sin of our first parents, Adam and Eve. In his infinite wisdom, however, God permitted this sin to happen and all of its harmful consequences, but because of his omnipotence and goodness he is able to draw good out of it. As St. Augustine said, God is so powerful that he can bring good out of evil.

Death as a Result of Sin

The biblical account of the origin of sin and death is contained in the first three chapters of Genesis. The inspired author here explains the source of the universal presence of sin and death in the human community. The Creator is infinitely good and powerful. If that is so, then how are we to explain the presence of evil and death in his creation? Something must have gone wrong at the beginning to distort his wise plan. God is portrayed as taking special care in the creation of the world and especially in the creation of Adam and Eve, the first man and woman and the first parents of the human race from whom we all descend. God breathed into them being and life and placed them in the garden of Paradise. In them, reason dominated the passions of the body and God made them immortal with a supernatural destiny in heaven. God is the living God and all life comes from him. So long as man remains subject to God, he shares in his life. But if he separates himself from the source of life, he will lose the gift of life. And that is what happened when Adam sinned against the command of God and followed the advice of Satan. As a result he separated himself from God, from the source of life, and fell under the power of suffering, corruption and death. He had been clearly warned, but he did not listen.

In a certain sense Adam represented all of us-all of his descendants. His sin brought disorder into the world because he separated himself from the source of all order and harmony. Because Adam represented all of us, we all are affected by his sin. The human nature we receive from him lacks something it should have, namely, a friendly relationship with the Creator that would have secured for us eternal life and immortality. The necessity of dying that is inherent in each one of us manifests not only that we are like the other animals, but also that we have been cut off from the principle of life.

The death of the human person, therefore, is essentially related to being separated from the living God. If man had been created mortal and not given a supernatural end, then the experience of death would not be unnatural and would not be evidence of separation from the divine will. But in the present order of divine providence, man's original immortality could not remain after the link with the divine will was broken because of sin.

Man was created immortal with a supernatural end. He did not lose that end as a result of his sin, but he did lose the grace that would enable him to attain that end. This is one of the reasons why man naturally shrinks from the prospect of death. We still have an ordination to eternal life. St. Thomas Aquinas, therefore, says that death is not natural to man, given that his soul is immortal and he will live forever, unlike all the other animals (STh I-II, 85, 6). The universal fear of death seems to manifest some kind of mental awareness that man is immortal and should not be subject to death and the disintegration of his body-spirit unity.

Death for the redeemed person in Christ is quite different from the death of the unredeemed sinner who lives on a natural plane without the grace of Christ. For the latter, death is a punishment not only for original sin but also for his own personal sins. By his own deliberate choices he has ratified his alienation from God that he inherited from Adam and his separation from God is made permanent in his death.

The death of the sinner is a certain triumph for the power of Satan, the enemy of God and the enemy of every human being who is created by God to take his place in heaven. There is always some connection between sin and the devil, not because Satan is behind every temptation—there is also the attraction of the world and the flesh. But his influence is there because the original sin of Adam and the loss of integrity and immortality did result from the devil's temptation; it is this lack of order or disharmony in man that continues to manifest itself in all subsequent refusals to serve God. Every sin is a continuation of man's rebellion against God and the sinner's death makes this permanent.[1]

Christ Changes the Meaning of Death

The Bible describes man's need of redemption in several different ways. He is said to be living in the shadow of death, to be a captive, to be in debt, to be living according to the flesh, to be wandering on the wrong road. These are various ways of saying that man, when separated from the living God, is dead in sin. These expressions are not restricted to the death of the body, but death as it affects the totality of the human person. Redemption

---

1   For a full treatment of the role of sin in the Bible see: William G. Heidt, O.S.B., "The Major Old Testament Theme," *Old Testament Reading Guide* #30 (Collegeville, MN: The Liturgical Press, 1968).

by Christ, therefore, means a change or transformation of man's mortal condition—a change from death to life.

God's plan to save man did not mean that he would do away with death and return man to his original state of immortality. The fact of the sin of Adam cannot be undone and its consequences remain. But God can change the internal meaning of death so that it leads man not away from God, but becomes the door or gateway to his eternal salvation. This change cannot be superficial or accidental; it must go to the very root or heart of death. This means that death must be changed so that it leads to everlasting life and not to eternal ruin and damnation.

The Death of Christ

In order to change the meaning of human death God sent his Son into the world "in the likeness of sinful flesh" (Rom 8:3). In the Incarnation the Son of God became flesh, became a mortal man and a son of Adam; sinless himself, he took to himself a human nature subject to suffering and death as a result of the first sin. Because of the malice, ignorance and hatred of some of his contemporaries he was crucified and put to death; he freely accepted his painful death in loving submission to the will of his Father as he expressed it in the Garden of Gethsemane, "not my will but thine be done" (Matt. 26:39). Death, so much feared and hated by sinful men, was now accepted in loving obedience to the Father and for the salvation of all mankind. It was the supreme sacrificial act of submission to make reparation for the rebellion of man. This loving gift of himself to the Father was accepted by the Father; the result was his glorious resurrection from the dead and his glory at the right hand of the Father. In Jesus death is swallowed up in victory, "captivity is led captive," and Jesus has changed the whole meaning of death. Death is no longer simply a sign of sin and rebellion against God. Now it is the doorway to heaven and eternal life and a sign of the power of God's love with regard to sinful men.[2]

By offering himself to the Father for our sake, as the New Adam and the eternal High Priest, Jesus was not acting as an

---

2   See CCC 1009.

individual but as the divinely appointed representative of the whole human race. He suffered death freely for us so that he might communicate his own grace and divine life to his fellow men. As St. Paul says, he was obedient unto death—even the death of the cross and because of that God exalted him and glorified him at his right hand; from there he sends out his Holy Spirit to sanctify those who believe in Jesus Christ (Phil 2:6–11). As the resurrected and glorified Lord, Jesus is the source of man's salvation and the source of the divine Spirit who makes us children of God and heirs of heaven. Because of Jesus' death in accordance with the will of the Father, the situation of fallen man in relation to God has been completely changed. Man no longer lives in the shadow of death, because the life and light of Christ shines on him. For one member of the human race— Jesus Christ both God and man—has triumphed over sin and death and entered into eternal life. In order to communicate that life to all mankind, he instituted his Church with its seven sacraments as channels of his grace to those who have faith in him.

Because of Jesus' death and resurrection the world as a whole and as the place of man's personal activity has become something completely different from what it would be if Christ had not died and risen from the dead. Because of his human reality and the infinite grace he merited for us, his death has changed the world and has changed the meaning of human death. Jesus Christ, with his life, death and resurrection, affects the innermost reality of the world. Because of his death and resurrection Christ has become, even in his humanity, what he already always was in dignity, "the Heart of the world" and the divine center of all created reality.[3]

The life of a Catholic is literally surrounded with things that remind him of the salvific death of Jesus. Here I will mention just a few of them. First of all there is the Holy Sacrifice of the Mass which is the re-presentation sacramentally, in an unbloody manner, of the sacrificial death of Jesus on Calvary 2,000 years ago. The Christ present in the Eucharist is the glorified Christ at the right hand of the Father, but the separate consecration of

---

3   For more information on this point see Karl Rahner, S.J., "Tod Jesu" in LThK 10, 231–232.

the bread and wine signifies and makes present the death of Jesus who poured out all of his love for us and for our salvation for the remission of sins. He told us to do this in memory of him. When we make the Sign of the Cross in the name of the Trinity we are affirming faith in the resurrected Jesus in heaven. When we look at the crucifix we see the dead body of Christ who died for love of us. The Stations of the Cross in every Catholic church remind us of the suffering and death of Our Lord. With regard to our own death in imitation of him, we mention it explicitly every time we pray the "Hail Mary" in the concluding words when we ask our Blessed Mother to "pray for us sinners now, and at the hour of our death. Amen." The liturgy of the Church offers us some beautiful prayers for the dead, especially in the Requiem Mass where we say in the Preface that, for the Christian, in death "life is changed, not ended."

The Death of a Christian

The death of a Christian believer, therefore, is very different from the death of a sinner who dies in Adam or of a pagan who does not know Christ. Death always remains for us obscure and mysterious because something basic happens to us in death and we do not know exactly what it is. But because of our salvation in Christ Jesus, death is no longer just a punishment for sin, since the Christian by his Baptism in Christ has been liberated from the power of sin. As St. Paul said in Rom. 8:1, there is nothing worthy of condemnation in the justified Christian. Theologians say rather that, after Christ, death is a negative consequence of sin. In his wisdom God has not abolished death after the redemption worked by Jesus on the cross. It is now a test of man's faith, hope and love of God and is to be accepted in humble obedience to the will of the Father in imitation of Jesus himself. Death is now the end of time and suffering and is the door to eternal life for those who die in Christ as St. Paul and all the saints have done.

The death of a Christian is the most important thing that will ever happen to him. His suffering during life, his prayer, his practice of virtue, his reception of the sacraments of the Church, his participation of the Holy Sacrifice of the Mass and his reception of Holy Communion—all of these things are preparation for the decisive moment of death when his continuing life for all eternity, either happy in heaven or miserable in hell, will be determined by the final judgment of Christ. This happens for each one of us only once—there is no second chance—there is no chance to have a change of mind as there is in this temporal life when we make a mistake and then take steps to correct it. "It is appointed for men once to die" (Heb. 9:27). Death is forever. In the Gospels Jesus warned us about this many times when he spoke about the punishment of hell, the joy of heaven and that he will come to call us unexpectedly and come to us like a thief in the night. Therefore he tells us to be always vigilant, to be ready for him at any time, for one day he will surely come to get us.

Death and the Grace of God

Man prepares himself for death and the next life by faith in Jesus Christ, by being an active member of the Church in receiving the sacraments regularly, by practicing the love of God and neighbor, in short, by living a supernatural life of virtue animated by the sanctifying grace of God. God has revealed his will for us in the Bible and the tradition of the Church. By faith we respond to his revelation and accept his word that by Baptism we are raised to the supernatural level and that we have a supernatural end. By faith man confidently directs himself to a goal that transcends the temporal and visible things of this mortal life.

There is an essential connection between Christian faith and death. Faith in Jesus Christ is the final and perfect answer to the problem of human mortality because of which the possibility and danger of death is with us every day of our life. For the Christian, death is the mysterious door through which he must pass in order to reach perfect human fulfillment and life without end. For the Christian, death is not defeat nor annihilation nor destruction. The experience of death for the believer means coming face to face with his loving and merciful Creator. It means the fullness of life and existence that he has always been striving for on earth but could never attain. St. Augustine uttered a basic truth about man when he said that our hearts were made for God and that they will never rest until they rest in God. Faith, grace and the sacraments give us the means to attain that glorious end. When we die, the obscurity of faith is transformed into clarity of vision and understanding by a special gift that the theologians call "the light of glory."

Since nothing unclean can appear before the all-holy God, the souls of those who die with unforgiven venial sins or the unpaid debt of punishment for forgiven sins must first go to purgatory where they will be detained and purified until they are ready to enter heaven. The souls in purgatory are suffering but they are also happy because they know they are saved and that they will surely enter heaven. Some years ago a pious elderly woman, who also had a difficult and irascible personality and was afraid she might commit a sin of anger, asked me to pray for her that she would soon die and go to purgatory. She said that if she went to purgatory she would be sure of her eternal salvation. That is a very Catholic attitude because it is suffused with hope in God's mercy.

The virtue of hope refers to the expectation that one has of achieving some good in the future. The hoped for good must be possible of attainment, but it is often also difficult to obtain. There are two kinds of hope—natural and supernatural. Natural hope means that we desire to obtain some future good by our own efforts or by some stroke of luck. Supernatural hope is an infused virtue that comes to us with our Baptism; it gives us the expectation of attaining our final end in heaven with the help of God's grace. This presupposes our final perseverance and dying in the state of sanctifying grace. Sins against hope are presumption and despair. Without the supernatural virtue of hope man sees death as meaningless and will face it with a sense of despair. For one who has faith in God's mercy and goodness death does not mean the end of life; rather, it means the beginning of a better life in which one's heart is completely filled with happiness.

Charity or the love of God is the greatest of all the virtues. The person who loves God with his whole heart, soul, mind and strength is united with him and participates in his divine life. The one who loves God in this way has already, in a certain sense, triumphed over death because he is united with God who is the fullness of life; he is the source of all life. As St. Peter said, "Lord, to whom can we go? You have the words of eternal life" (John 6:68). The love of God is stronger than death. For one who loves God, the moment of death is the act by which he delivers his soul to the loving care of God the Father. In her last moments St. Thérèse of Lisieux, the young Carmelite saint, said, "I am not dying; I am entering life."[4]

Death and the Seven Sacraments

The grace that Jesus Christ merited for us by his passion, death and resurrection is channeled to us in a visible way through the seven sacraments which are the visible signs of invisible grace instituted by Christ and entrusted to his Church. The graces communicated to the Christian believer through each of the sacraments strengthen the spiritual life of the soul and prepare it for the eternal life that will be his after the experience of temporal death. So all of the sacraments are related to death in some way. Baptism is the sacrament of regeneration through water and the word. It is a rebirth into the life of God and a participation in the death of Christ. In Baptism one passes from the death of sin to the life of God by being sacramentally buried and raised with Christ (see John 3:5; Rom. 6:1–4). As a result the baptized person becomes a friend of God and a new creature. In Baptism the paschal mystery of Christ is applied to children of Adam who are infected with original sin and transforms them from children of wrath to members of the kingdom of God. The Holy Spirit is given to the new Christian as a promise and pledge of eternal life after the sufferings of this life for those who remain faithful and persevere in the grace of God. So Baptism is the beginning of a pilgrimage that ends with physical death and the beginning of eternal life with God and all the angels and saints.

Confirmation is the sacrament of spiritual strengthening through a special conferral of the Holy Spirit for those who have already been baptized. "To confirm" means to strengthen, so

4   The quote is given in CCC 1011.

Confirmation is often referred to as the "Sacrament of Maturity." In the Acts of the Apostles we see how the Apostles on Pentecost were suddenly changed from rather timid, fearful individuals to fearless preachers of the Good News of Jesus Christ. In the power of that Spirit they went on to die as martyrs for the faith. Through the gift of the Holy Spirit the confirmed Christian is sent into the world to be a witness in word and deed to the presence of the kingdom of God to be found in the Catholic Church. The ultimate witness, of course, is to die for the faith as a martyr—like Saints Isaac Jogues, John de Brebeuf and the other North American martyrs in the 17th century or like Maximilian Kolbe in the 20th century. Not all are called to make this ultimate sacrifice as a witness to the faith, but all should be prepared by prayer and the sacraments for this sacrifice, if it should be God's will for them. Most Christians are called by God to give witness in their ordinary daily life by their words and good deeds that are a manifestation of their faith. They do this in a striking way by accepting in advance the death that God chooses to send them, especially those who are diagnosed with a terminal disease. Every Christian who dies in Christ gives witness to his faith and fulfills the task given to him when he received the Holy Spirit in Confirmation.

There is an essential connection between the Eucharist and death because the holy Sacrifice of the Mass is, as the Council of Trent declared, an unbloody re-presentation of the death of Jesus on the cross 2,000 years ago. Because of Jesus' death on the cross for our sake we have the Holy Eucharist. That death is re-enacted by the separate consecration of the bread and wine into the body and blood of Christ. Jesus instituted the Eucharist during the Last Supper on the day before he died. He told his Apostles and those who would believe in him to do this in memory of him. When we receive Jesus in the Eucharist we share in the life of the glorified Christ and receive his pledge of eternal life. The Eucharist contains a promise of victory over death through the almighty power of Jesus, for he said: "He who eats my flesh and drinks my blood has eternal life, and I will raise him up on the last day" (John 6:54). When the time of death arrives, faithful Catholics want to receive the Holy Eucharist which, at this time, is called "Viaticum" because it means that Jesus keeps company with the dying person on the way to eternity. The Eucharist has often been referred to as "the medicine of immortality" and "the antidote for death."[5] It is food and strengthening for the difficult journey through death to eternal life with the Holy Trinity.

Penance is the sacrament instituted by Christ by which sins committed after Baptism are forgiven through confession to a priest and the reception of absolution. This sacrament was given to the Church by Our Lord on the day of his resurrection when he breathed on his apostles and said to them: "Receive the Holy Spirit. If you forgive the sins of any, they are forgiven; if you retain the sins of any, they are retained" (John 20:22–23). Through mortal sin a person loses sanctifying grace, the life of the soul, and falls into a state of spiritual death. Penance restores the life of grace and makes one again pleasing to God. In addition to forgiving sins, the sacrament also communicates grace to help the individual to avoid sin in the future. It is a participation in the death of Christ to sin. Penance removes some of the temporal punishment due to sin in purgatory and prepares one to accept the death that the Lord may send him sooner or later. Death itself, accepted from God in faith and love, is a form of penance and satisfaction for past sins. Before Vatican II, after the absolution, the priest offered a prayer over the penitent to remind him to offer his good works and sufferings daily to the Lord in reparation for past sins and to gain further grace: "May the passion of our Lord Jesus Christ, the merits of the Blessed Virgin Mary and of all the saints, and whatever good you do and evil you endure, be cause to you for the remission of your sins, the increase of grace, and the reward of everlasting life. Amen." But one attains everlasting life by passing through the mystery of death of which we all have a natural fear. So the Sacrament of Penance which removes mortal sin, the death of the soul, is intimately related to physical death and prepares one to meet it with faith, hope and love.

It is difficult to be good when one is sick and dying. Dying persons are often attacked by the devil with serious temptations against faith and belief in a loving God. In order to help man in

5   CCC 1405.

his last hours Our Lord instituted the Sacrament of the Anointing of the Sick which used to be called "Extreme Unction" because it is usually the last anointing before one passes through death from this world of time to the next world of eternity. Just as Confirmation is the perfection of Baptism, so Anointing of the Sick is the perfection of Penance. Vatican II clarified that the sacrament is not just for those who are at the point of death, but also for those who are seriously sick and *may be* exposed to death. The Council said: "The anointing of the sick is not a sacrament for those only who are at the point of death. Hence as soon as any of the faithful begins to be in danger of death from sickness or old age, the appropriate time for him to receive this sacrament has certainly already arrived."[6] The grace conferred through the sacrament strengthens both body and soul, removes the temporal punishment due to past sins, and enables one to share in the passion and death of Jesus. If at all possible, the sacrament should be given while the person is still conscious so he or she can join in the prayers. St. James said that the elders should pray over the sick person and anoint him with oil: "The prayer of faith will save the sick man, and the Lord will raise him up; and if he has committed sins, he will be forgiven" (James 5:14–15). On this same point Vatican II said: "By the anointing of the sick and the prayer of her priests, the whole Church commends those who are ill to the suffering and glorified Lord, asking that he may lighten their suffering and save them. She exhorts them, however…to associate themselves freely with the passion and death of Christ."[7] So through this sacrament Christ comes with his powerful grace to the dying person to help him to reject the devil, to accept God's will in his regard, and to commit himself completely into the hands of his loving Creator. Because of his merciful love Jesus gave us this "sacrament of the dying" to help us to face death and accept it as God's will for us and the entrance to eternal life.

The Sacraments of Holy Orders and Matrimony are sometimes referred to as the social sacraments or the sacraments of vocation. Matrimony contributes to the increase in the numbers

6   Vatican II, *Constitution on the Sacred Liturgy*, #73.
7   Vatican II, *Dogmatic Constitution on the Church*, #11.

of the faithful and has as one of its main purposes the creation of new immortal persons who will become members of the Mystical Body of Christ and destined for eternal life. Matrimony provides more guests at the table of eternal life. The purpose of Holy Orders is to provide priests and bishops who will preach the word of God and administer the Seven Sacraments. They are channels of grace for the faithful to assist them to live a full Christian life and to get to heaven when they pass from this world to the next. These two sacraments may not be directly related to the mystery of death, but they certainly are related to it at least in an indirect way since both prepare people to die in the Lord and so to attain eternal salvation in the kingdom of God.[8]

Entrance into the Kingdom of Heaven

Death in the state of sanctifying grace as a member of the mystical body of Christ is the beginning of eternal life for the Christian. It is his entrance into the kingdom of heaven where he will remain in happiness for all eternity. Being in Christ in faith and love in this life is the beginning of eternal life and the possession of the Holy Spirit is the pledge of future glory that is attained through death in Christ.

In this life the possession of the grace of Christ is always questionable, since man is afflicted with the consequence of original sin which is called "concupiscence." This means that man has an attraction towards sin and it is difficult for him to control his passions and always to be seeking the will of God in all things. Since man's will is free, in this life there is always the possibility of rebelling against God and falling into mortal sin. Death changes all of this. After death when the person sees God clearly he is confirmed in goodness and cannot fall away from it because his will is confirmed in goodness. He is united to Christ as a member of his body forever. The soul looks forward to the final coming of the kingdom and the resurrection of the

8   This analysis of the relation between the sacraments and death is based on the article "Death, Theology of" by J. H. Wright in the *New Catholic Encyclopedia*, Vol. 4., 687–695.

body when Christ will come again in glory at the end of the world.

In death the Christian is separated from relatives and friends on this earth, but he enters into another dimension of the Communion of Saints—whether in purgatory or in heaven. By being a member of the Body of Christ he enters into a new relationship with all those who are animated by the grace and life of Christ. Christian death is the beginning of an intimate union in knowledge and love with Christ and with all of those who are in Christ. Also, when one has passed from this life of tribulation to the next life of bliss the individual has a new relationship to those on earth who have not yet passed through the door of death to life everlasting. Many prayers in the liturgy of the Church assure is that the saints in heaven pray for us and intercede for us before the throne of God. Some have extraordinary influence with God, especially the Blessed Virgin Mary and St. Joseph.

There is a close connection between death and the resurrection of the body. Once the soul has left the body in the act of death it is no longer tied to material things and living in the obscurity of faith. Now with the grace of the Beatific Vision it can see God; now it knows clearly and fully the truth about God, man and the world; now it enjoys the fullness of supernatural life in God. The soul transformed by the divine life can now be used by the infinite power of Christ to raise the body from the dead. This will happen at the end of the world when Christ comes again in glory to judge the living and the dead. In the resurrection, the body will be glorified by the power of the glorified soul and will be totally subject to the soul. It will be like the resurrected body of Christ on Easter Sunday with unheard of powers of passing through walls, appearing and disappearing as the resurrected person wishes. There will be no suffering and no death. As St. Paul said: "When the perishable puts on the imperishable, and the mortal puts on immortality, then shall come to pass the saying that is written: 'Death is swallowed up in victory'" (1 Cor. 15:54; Isa. 25:8; Hos. 13:14). Then we will understand and appreciate completely the wisdom of God is allowing us to pass from this temporal world filled with trials and tribulations through death to his everlasting kingdom of heaven.

CHAPTER 4:
THEOLOGY OF DEATH

The wages of sin is death, but the free gift of God is eternal life
in Christ Jesus our Lord. (Rom. 6:23)

We have seen that the human soul is immortal, but man's life on this earth in time is mortal. The Bible says that the life of man is three score and ten years, and four score for those who are strong (Ps. 90). After a long or a short life each person must die; after death the body disintegrates into the elements out of which it was made, but the soul lives on in eternity. We have seen that death is a consequence of sin; for the soul that dies in the state of mortal sin it means damnation and separation from God; for the soul that dies in the state of grace death means entry into heaven and the face to face vision of God, unless detained for a period of purification in purgatory. Those who are saved are saved by the grace of Jesus Christ communicated to them through faith and the sacraments.[1]

Philosophers and thinkers of all kinds have tried to answer the questions: What is the purpose or meaning of human existence? Where did man come from and where is he going? Why are we here on this planet? Many false answers to these questions have been given. As Catholics and as believers in the divinity of Jesus Christ we know the correct answers to these questions. You can find them in the *Catechism of the Catholic Church* or in any of the older catechisms. The answers have been given to us by God himself and are contained in the Bible which is the word of God which is infallibly true and therefore reliable.

---

1   For more details on this see: J. H. Wright, "Death, Theology of," *New Catholic Encyclopedia*, Vol. 4, 687–695. In future references *New Catholic Encyclopedia* will be abbreviated to NCE.

The Catholic Church founded by Jesus 2,000 years ago and headed by the Pope, who is the Vicar of Christ, tells us with infallible authority what the correct answers to the questions are. God created me and he created me to know, love and serve him in this life and to be happy with him forever in the next life. If I do what I am supposed to do, if I follow God's commandments then on the day of my death I will be his friend and he will welcome me into eternal happiness with the Holy Trinity and all the angels and saints. In short, the whole purpose of life is final union with God in love; that will make a person perfectly happy forever.

We know from revelation and the teaching of the Church that this temporary life on earth is a time of probation and testing; now we are pilgrims and travelers on our way to eternal life. Our time of probation will end with our death. Those who die in the grace of God because they have led a life of love of God and neighbor will be judged favorably by Jesus and will go to heaven immediately, unless they have to be purified for a time in purgatory. Those who have rejected God's commandments and have lived a life of selfishness, have chosen themselves or some material thing in the place of God, and because they have so freely chosen die as enemies of God and so will be sent immediately to a place that is separated from God; that is what the Bible and the Church mean by damnation or hell.

What we want to consider here is the role that death plays with regard to the eternal destiny of each human person. From what we have seen it is clear that death is the key or decisive moment in the life of each individual. Death is the end of the time of probation and testing; it is the end of the time during which man can choose to serve God and save his soul or to turn away from his Creator as his last end, having put some creature in the place of God as the final purpose of his existence. After death man's status is fixed and cannot be changed—either for happiness or misery, depending on whether or not he died as a friend or an enemy of God.[2]

---

2   Thomas Aquinas explains why the human will cannot change after death in *Summa Contra Gentiles* 4, 91–95. In future references the *Summa* will be abbreviated to SCG.

At this point theologians ask why death is the decisive event in the life of each human person. What is there about death that makes it either the beginning of eternal happiness in heaven or the beginning of a miserable existence in hell cut off from all that is good and beautiful?

An important point to remember in this difficult question is that there is something definitive about death. Man's whole existence is changed, since the soul after death is now separated from the body in time and space which is the source of its intrinsic changeableness. Since our life in time is one of testing and probation, what we are at death is what we shall be for all eternity. What we are at death is a summation of all our previous free acts. One is either living in conformity with the will of God or he is not. After death there is no possibility of change— there is no second chance, as there is in this life. Why is that? St. Thomas gives the reason: "souls immediately after their separation from the body become unchangeable in will, with the result that the will of man cannot further be changed, neither from good to evil, nor from evil to good."[3] Because man's will is immutable after death, there can be no such thing as a free option for God after death, so that one who died in the state of grace might turn away from God, or one who died in the state of mortal sin might change his mind and make an act of perfect love of God and so attain eternal salvation.

Proof for the immutability of the will after death is given by Our Lord in his parable of the Last Judgment in Matt. 25:31– 46. The eternal lot of those who die is determined by what they did in this life: "Come, O blessed of my Father...I was hungry and you gave me food....Depart from me, you cursed, into the eternal fire...for I was hungry and you gave me no food....And they will go away into eternal punishment, but the righteous into eternal life." A second proof for the immutability of the will after death is found in the Church teaching that all baptized infants, who do not have the use of reason and cannot make any free acts for or against God, go directly to heaven and attain eternal salvation.[4] Another indication is that the Holy Innocents

3   SCG 4, 92.
4   D 857–858.

killed by King Herod are honored as saints and their feast is celebrated right after Christmas on December 28. That could not be if it were possible for some of them to reject God and so not go to heaven. We find confirmation of this truth also in St. Paul who said: "For all the truth about us will be brought out in the law court of Christ, and each of us will be what he deserves *for the things he did in the body, good or bad*" (2 Cor. 5:10, emphasis added; see also Matt. 25:34ff.; Luke 16:26; John 9:4).

In her opposition to the view of Origen and some of his followers regarding the possible or eventual conversion and salvation of those in hell after a long period of punishment, the Church has clearly taught that those in heaven are confirmed in glory and cannot lose it, and that those in hell are confirmed in hatred of God and cannot change.

In modern times some Catholic theologians have held that at the moment of death the soul can make a choice or option for or against God. If this were so it would mean that those who die in the state of mortal sin could have a change of mind after death and make an act of perfect love of God that would bring about their eternal salvation. It would also mean that those who have lived a good life and been obedient to God's will could, after their death, change their mind and turn themselves away from God. The intention of these thinkers is laudable in the sense that they realize the horror of eternal damnation for anyone and they would like to find a way to make it possible for dying sinners to be saved. The problem with this is that there is no support for it in Scripture or the tradition of the Church; various forms of this over the centuries have been proposed by the Origenists, but they have been condemned by the Church on several occasions.

There are further questions about why death is the decisive moment for each individual in determining his eternal status as either blessedly happy in heaven through the vision of God, or eternally miserable in hell in a state of alienation from God and hatred for him like Satan and his devils. One opinion about this is that it is simply the will of God that death should be the point at which one's eternal destiny is determined. Some have held that God, who is supremely free, could have established some other event or choice as the determining factor, and that he could have allowed souls through free choices to merit and de-merit after death. The point of these theologians is that there is nothing intrinsic to the nature of death why it should be the de-cisive moment that determines man's happiness or misery in the next life.

Such an explanation does not seem to be sufficient. God is supremely free and so he was free to create or not to create; he was free to become man and so provide a means of eternal sal-vation for the descendants of Adam born in original sin. But as Pope Benedict XVI has said, God is supreme intelligence and operates in a rational way. When he creates something, such as the world or man, he gives it a certain nature and in his dealings with it he respects that nature. There is nothing capricious about God and his dealings with the world and with man. So if death is the decisive, determining moment and event for man's eter-nal destiny, there must be some intrinsic reason for that rooted in the very nature of man. As we have seen, man's earthly life is a time of testing and probation to prepare him for eternal life since man's soul is immortal. Whatever God does, has a pur-pose and that purpose is always good because he is infinite goodness. The ultimate purpose of man is to get to heaven and live happily in God's presence forever. So there must be some-thing about death itself that in God's wisdom is the reason why it is the decisive moment with regard to man's eternal future.

It is not sufficient to say that sinners cannot change their mind after death merely because God does not will to give them the grace to do it. In some way death itself must be the reason why sinners are confirmed in their rejection of God in such a way that God's grace does not reach them, not because God re-jects them, but because they have rejected God and will not ac-cept his grace. Just as the damned cannot change, so also the saved can no longer merit and increase their love for God and so attain a higher place in heaven. The point is that the human soul after death is immutably fixed either for God or against him. So it must be something in the nature of death itself that makes it the decisive moment and not some free decision of God that has no relation to it.

To discover why death is the decisive act or event to deter-mine man's eternity, it is necessary to reflect on the nature of man as he operates in this life as a spirit in matter, with special emphasis on his freedom and his free choices. For praise and blame of man depend on what he freely chooses to do or not to do. Moral merit and demerit depend on what is voluntary. Man's relation to God and eternity is determined by the free choices he makes in this life; they flow from his nature as a spirit in matter, but also as one influenced by divine grace. St. Paul tells us that God desires the salvation of all (1 Tim. 2:4); this means that he also gives sufficient grace to all in this life to be saved.

The natural condition of man in this life is very changeable. The body in space and time is constantly changing as one progresses from childhood to maturity to old age. Circumstances, surroundings, persons keep changing; man lives in time and time marches on. Man develops habits and attains maturity by making many different choices. He can change from good to evil and from evil to good. In this life no one is confirmed in goodness to such an extent that he cannot change his mind. There is always the possibility that a holy person will have a change of mind and commit a serious sin and that a sinner will repent and turn back to God. That is why the Lord tells us to watch and pray that we enter not into temptation.

Once the soul, however, is separated from the body in death its situation is very different. The soul, which is intellect and will, is no longer subject to the mutability of matter and the body. Therefore the state of the soul at the time of death—oriented towards love of God or to love of self—is fixed and cannot change. If one dies in Christ, his whole being is directed to Christ in faith, hope and love; if one dies rejecting Christ and putting self or some creature in the place of God, then he will be separated from God and will spend eternity in misery and hatred of God. The purpose of the Church is to help people become members of Christ's body and to die in the state of grace. Therefore the Church insists on the importance of conferring the Sacraments of Penance, Anointing of the Sick and Holy Communion or Viaticum to those who are about to die. The purpose is to make sure that the soul of the dying person is in the state of sanctifying grace when he goes to meet Jesus, his Eternal Judge, so that he will be saved and go to heaven. In

Church teaching and tradition there is no thought or suggestion that a person who dies with the sacraments of the Church might reject God after his death and so choose hell rather than heaven. Because of its previous life and dying in the grace of God, the soul has chosen God for all eternity and that choice is made final by his death.

Scripture and the teaching of the Church affirm that a person is judged by Christ and his eternal destiny of heaven or hell is determined by his good or bad actions freely performed while the soul was united to the body in this mortal life in which the soul acts in dependence on the body. We have already mentioned that St. Paul said Christ will judge "according to what each one has done in the body" (2 Cor. 5:10). Our Lord has warned us about being ready *now and in this life* so that we will be sure of salvation: "Watch, therefore, for you do not know in what day your Lord is coming....you must be ready; for the Son of Man is coming at an hour you do not expect" (Matt. 24:42, 44; also 25:13; Mark 13:35, 37; Luke 12:40). Why would Our Lord, who knows all things, be so insistent that one be a friend of God before death, if he could still save himself by a free act in the next life? The theory, therefore, of some theologians that souls have an opportunity after death to make a free option in favor of God or against him has no support in Scripture, Tradition or the Magisterium of the Church.

We conclude, therefore, that the soul's state of immutability after death flows from the nature of death as the final separation of the soul from the body and the material world of time and space. What a man is at death as the result of all his previous life and choices determines his eternal future either of happiness in the presence of God or misery in the presence of Satan. That is why it is so important that one die in the state of sanctifying grace which is the divine life of the soul and pledge of future glory. In this perspective, we can say that all of one's free choices while alive on this earth in one way or another are a preparation for the crucial act of dying. The person who lives a life of virtue, receives the Sacraments regularly, keeps the Ten Commandments and practices the love of God and neighbor is preparing himself to die as a member of God's family and the communion of saints. On the other hand, one who rejects God's law and makes a little god of himself or some bodily pleasure like sex, riches, fame or power is preparing himself to die as an enemy of God who will be separated from God for all eternity to be punished in hell. It is hard for us to imagine that anyone could deliberately make such a choice, but Jesus mentions the reality of hell and damnation at least thirty times in the Gospels. Therefore, in this time of probation hell always remains a real possibility for all of us because we always remain free to turn our backs on God. For this reason St. Paul told his beloved Philippians to work out their salvation "in fear and trembling" (Phil. 2:12).

Regarding the future life of immortal human souls, in 1336 Pope Benedict XII in the dogmatic constitution *Benedictus Deus* made a significant declaration about the future lot of those who die in the state of grace and those who die in mortal sin: "We define that...the souls of all the saints who departed from this world, *soon after their death* and...purification...have been, are and will be in heaven....Moreover, we define that...the souls of those who die in actual mortal sin go down into hell *soon after their death.*"[5] From this it is clear that the time of deciding for or against God is during this life and not after death—the separation of the soul from the body.

Human life, since it is mortal, is constantly exposed to the possibility of death from the first moment of conception. The possibility and danger of death is recognized by all of us daily when we greet someone by saying, "How are you?" The implication is that the person could be sick and thus in danger of death. When a friend gets into a car we say, "Drive safely." Again, the implication is that the individual could be injured or killed while driving a car. Life insurance is based on the future reality of death. Health food, organic food, vitamins, eating oatmeal to reduce cholesterol—these things are all related to extending life and warding off the inevitability of death. The same can be said for the hundreds of billions of dollars spent each year on hospitals, doctors, surgery and medicine. All of that is related to man's mortality.

Modern philosophers and theologians have pointed out that all of our free choices in the course of life are related to

5   D 1000–1002; emphasis added.

death and fulfilled in death. What we are as a person at any given moment is the result of all the free choices we have made in the past. Thus, the soul's state at the moment of death is already anticipated in a certain way in the free choices that preceded it. What we are during life is what we shall be at the moment of death. That is why all of our free choices are so important. Voluntary acts are either moral or immoral and it is they that will determine whether we go to heaven or to hell. Each free act is irrevocable in the sense that it cannot be undone and the results remain with us. Good acts make us good and virtuous, while evil acts make us bad and loaded with vices or bad habits.

The anticipated presence of death in our free acts lends great importance to them. The sufferings and trials of life, the joys and the sorrows prepare us for the crucial moment when we die and our soul leaves the body and this world of time and space. Then it enters into God's timeless world of eternity. A life of virtue, self-sacrifice and love, in union with Jesus Christ, who suffered and died for my sake and my salvation, prepares one for entrance into the kingdom of God and everlasting happiness. That is the end for which God created me in the first place. Jesus has shown us the way. It is spelled out clearly in the four Gospels. Jesus is the Way, the Truth and the Life (John 14:6). By imitating him and following him we have an infallible guide and travel on the road to final personal fulfillment and eternal bliss.

Death is the final, fulfilling event of human life. One dies as one has lived. The first appearance of death was a punishment for sin when Adam rebelled against God and lost his preternatural immortality. By dying on the cross for love of us Jesus Christ, God and Man, changed the nature of death. Surely, death is natural to man but now, because of Jesus, it is the gateway to eternal life. Jesus was the perfect man who had the immediate vision of God. But for love of us he assumed a weak human nature that was subject to suffering and death. By dying he destroyed our death and by rising in his resurrection he restored our life—the life of the soul given to us through faith and the sacraments. Seated at the right hand of the Father in glory he sends out the Holy Spirit to all those who have faith in him.

The Catholic who imitates Christ and strives to live in union with him through a life of prayer and reception of the sacraments by that very fact accepts in advance as a sign of God's will the death God decreed for him in his providence. In this acceptance he unites himself with the death of Jesus himself who died in accordance with the will of the Father. His whole life as a faithful Christian reaches its summit and fulfillment in his death with Christ. By dying with Christ he enters into eternity to join the communion of the blessed and with them looks forward to the end of this world and the Second Coming of Christ in glory and the resurrection of the body. When the soul has been reunited to the glorified body the human person has reached his final perfection and is able to offer worthy praise, glory and honor to the Holy Trinity forever for the wonders of creation and redemption.[6]

6   The arrangement of some of the material in this chapter is indebted to the article on "Death, Theology of" by J. H. Wright in NCE, Vol. 4, 687–695; also consulted were Karl Rahner, "Tod" in LThK 10, 218–226 and "De Novissimis" in *Sacrae Theologiae Summa* IV (BAC 1956), 866–877.

CHAPTER 5:
PREPARATION FOR DEATH

Behold, now is the acceptable time; behold,
now is the day of salvation. (2 Cor. 6:2)

The wise man is the one who prepares for his future. That is easy to understand when it comes to making the necessary provisions for food, drink, clothing and shelter. There are many statements in the Bible about the difference between the wise and foolish person. The spiritually wise person is the one who prepares himself for a happy eternity in the presence of God and with all the angels and saints; he prepares himself by showing reverence for God and keeping his commandments. Our Lord tells us in the Gospels to watch and pray that we do not enter into temptation. He also says that he will come to get us at a time we do not expect, like a thief in the night. The Bible, and especially the New Testament, abounds in warnings about being prepared to meet our Eternal Judge when we die and pass from this temporal life to eternal life. Our Lord tells us to "watch and pray" and St. Paul tells us to "pray always." Every sincere and humble prayer is a preparation for death because it puts us in conformity with God's will and makes us ready to accept that will—whatever it may be. Every act of religion and every act of worship of God is, in its own way, at least implicitly, preparation for death and eternal union with God.

There are hundreds of good books by saints, theologians and serious Catholics that tell us how to pray and how to prepare ourselves to pass through death successfully so that we get to heaven and attain the goal for which we were created. The most important book, of course, is the Bible which contains the word of God, especially the New Testament with the four Gospels. In addition to that we have the writings of the Fathers of the Church and spiritual classics such as the *Summa Theologiae* of St. Thomas Aquinas, and the spiritual writings of great saints like Teresa of Avila, John of the Cross, Francis de Sales, Ignatius Loyola, and Thérèse of Lisieux. After the Bible one of the most important sources of spiritual guidance is *The Imitation of Christ* by Thomas à Kempis. Hundreds of more recent books are spinoffs or re-presentations of the ideas and practical advice contained in these classics. The main point of all these books is to teach us how to achieve union with God in this life and so prepare ourselves for heaven before we die, since being in the state of sanctifying grace thus sharing in the life of Christ is a pledge or ticket to eternal life. If the Holy Trinity dwells within our heart at the moment of death, then we are assured of the Beatific Vision and eternal happiness when we reach the other side. Nothing, absolutely nothing is more important than that.

Jesus Christ, the Second Person in the Holy Trinity, destroyed the power of Satan, sin and death by his sacrificial death on the cross. That death is re-presented sacramentally hundreds of thousands of times daily by Masses offered around the world for the worship of God and the salvation of souls. This means that death has taken on a new meaning because God himself, in his human nature, suffered death in order to merit grace and eternal life for us. It is because of the death of Jesus that we lead a supernatural life and have the happiness of heaven as our final goal. By uniting ourselves with Jesus through faith and Baptism we share in his victory over death. As St. Paul says in Romans 6, by Baptism we share in the death and resurrection of Christ. Christ has removed much of the terror and anxiety connected with death because we know for sure, through faith in him and hope and love, that if we are members of his Mystical Body death means a change from temporal life to eternal life. This idea is repeated in various ways in the funeral liturgy of the Church.

Because man is mortal in his very nature, death is a constant threat throughout his earthly life. This means that death can come any time and in any place. There is no such thing as complete protection against death. Every day we hear about people who die in a car crash, in an airplane accident, as a result of fire, from a sudden heart attack, by falling from a ladder, by drowning, and now often as victims of a terrorist attack. Man is here today and gone tomorrow (see 1 Macc. 2:63). And when he is out of sight, he is very soon out of mind. This being the case, Scripture and the saints urge us to be prepared each day to die and to meet our maker. Sleep is like a symbol of death. Someone has said that a bed is the most dangerous place to be, since most people die in bed. Accordingly, it is a good idea to pray before going to sleep with words something like this: "O Lord, into thy hands I commend my spirit."

Modern man is preoccupied with material things—the things of this world. Our secularist culture concentrates on the present and the importance of getting as much pleasure from it as one can. No thought is given to what happens to each individual after he or she dies. The emphasis is on the NOW. Killing and death are in the news every day, but this is reported as merely a fact that has affected others. Our secular culture does not like to think about the reality and meaning of death—(1) that all must die, and (2) the fate of the souls of those who die and leave this world. Secularists tend to ignore the spiritual reality and the immortality of the soul. Materialists and atheists, of course, simply deny the existence of any spiritual reality. For them nothing exists except matter and so the human soul is not immortal—it simply ceases to exist when death arrives. Therefore, for them, there is no personal existence after death—when a person dies he or she simply ceases to exist, so there is no point in worrying about one's fate after death. A practical consequence of this view is "eat, drink and be merry for tomorrow you will die." This is an attitude towards life that is dominant in the secular media.

The faithful Catholic does not share that view. He knows from the first page of the Catechism that he was made for God and that his ultimate destiny after this life, after he dies, is to be with God forever. Therefore the Catholic should often think about his absolute future which will be permanent after this life of constant change. As St. Augustine said at the beginning of his famous *Confessions*, "Our hearts were made for thee, O God, and they will not rest until they rest in thee." Man was not made primarily for this world but for the next world. How foolish it is for a man to totally immerse himself in this passing world and fail to prepare himself for the next world that lasts forever. The Bible tells us that the man is blessed who always has the hour of his death before his eyes and every day is prepared to die (see Sirach 7:40).

If God does not exist, of course, as the atheists claim, then there is no need to prepare oneself for death since, according to them, there is nothing after death—no personal survival, no heaven, no hell. Nothing. But if God does exists and the soul is immortal, then what happens to each person after he dies becomes very important. Blaise Paschal (1623–1662), the brilliant French mathematician, scientist and apologist for Catholicism reflected on this problem. He was familiar with the "Five Ways" of St. Thomas Aquinas to prove by reason the existence of God (STh I, 2, 1). Being a creative genius and an innovative mathematician, he was fascinated with probabilities and the odds involved in betting on horses and sporting events. He thought a lot about the existence of God and how to prove it. So he added to the Five Ways of St. Thomas his own "proof" in the form of a wager based on the odds of whether or not God exists.

Paschal's famous wager goes like this: God either exists or he does not exist, so I must of necessity lay odds for or against his existence, since I have free choice and in such an important matter cannot remain neutral. If I wager *for* God, and God exists—then I have an infinite gain. However, if God does not exist, then there is no loss.

If I wager *against* God, and God exists—then I will suffer an infinite loss. However, if God does not exist, then there is neither loss nor gain. In this second alternative I find myself in a situation wherein I am exposed to the loss of everything. Self-interest and human shrewdness, therefore, considering the odds, tell me that the wise choice is to make the wager that insures my winning everything or, at worst, losing nothing. It is to my advantage, therefore to wager that God exists and to live accordingly.

Paschal's proof is based on probabilities and the common human experience of order and beauty in the world that needs a reasonable explanation. For persons who want to win, especially to win an eternal reward, Paschal's Wager is definitely attractive. The person who chooses for God's existence and lives according to his rules is making a wise preparation for his eventual death. He has everything to win and nothing to lose.

The best way to prepare for death is to lead the life of a good Catholic by attending Mass every Sunday, going to confession regularly, praying every day and fulfilling the obligations of one's state in life. Devotion to the Sacred Heart of Jesus and daily recitation of the Rosary of the Blessed Virgin Mary are highly recommended to us by the Church and are signs that one is destined for eternal life, especially if one has made the nine First Fridays requested by Jesus in his revelations to St. Margaret Mary Alacoque. The purpose of these sacraments and prayers is to increase the virtues of faith, hope and love that lead to personal union and communion with God. St. Ignatius Loyola said that a goal of the spiritual life is "to find God in all things." When one has reached that stage, he or she is prepared for the mystery of death and the passage from this mortal life to unending life with all the angels and saints.

St. Thomas Aquinas said that meditation on the Passion of Christ is a good way to prepare oneself for death because by his suffering he merited the grace that is communicated to us through the Sacraments (see STh III, 61, 1 ad 3). Each of the Sacraments in its own way helps to prepare us to face death with a minimum of fear. That is because they increase our love for Christ and love strives for union. Through Baptism we die to sin and this world and are raised sacramentally with Christ (see Rom. 6:3–4; Col 3:3). Confirmation perfects Baptism and gives us the help of the Holy Spirit to strengthen us in facing the difficulties of life and to accept the death that God may send us. The Eucharist is a re-presentation of the death of the Lord on Calvary in which we share by receiving him worthily. Every time we attend Mass we are reminded of the death of the Lord and his glorious resurrection.

Mortal sin is followed by a sense of guilt and fear of eternal punishment. That fear is removed by the Divine Mercy available to us through the Sacrament of Penance. Marriage teaches one to love spouse and children; it is a great remedy for selfishness and in its own way prepares one for death. Holy Orders makes a man an ambassador for Christ and an instrument in his hands. The priest is called to lead a life of dedication and sacrifice for others. Daily he comes in personal contact with the death of the Lord when he offers the Holy Sacrifice of the Mass; each time he does that he is preparing himself eventually to die with the Lord and for the Lord. The Anointing of the Sick was instituted by Jesus especially for those who are at the door of death; it forgives their sins and strengthens them with special graces to accept death with faith, hope and love and to overcome final temptations of the devil. This Sacrament helps one to overcome the fear of death. Let us listen to the words of St. James on this Sacrament: "The prayer of faith will save the sick man, and the Lord will raise him up; and if he has committed sins, he will be forgiven" (James 5:15).

After Our Blessed Mother, St. Joseph is the most powerful saint in heaven. He has been named by the Church as the patron of a happy death. In Catholic thinking a "happy death" does not mean a painless death when one has been drugged into senselessness by morphine: that seems to be the understanding of the phrase in the secular world that is now advocating and practicing physician-assisted suicide. A happy death in the Catholic sense means that one dies in the grace of God, and hopefully also with the last Sacraments of the Church.

We pray to the Blessed Virgin Mary for help in all sorts of trials. Favorite prayers of many Catholics are the "Memorare" composed by St. Bernard of Clairveaux, and of course the "Hail Mary" which, after the "Our Father," is the prayer most often said by Catholics. Please note that every time we pray the "Hail Mary" we make reference to our own death and we ask her assistance that it may be a happy death: "Holy Mary, Mother of God, pray for us sinners now *and at the hour of our death. Amen.*" When we are dying we need all the help we can get and Our Lady is recognized as our most powerful intercessor before the throne of God.

The Particular Judgment after Death

Immediately after death each person will be judged by Jesus Christ on the basis of his good and bad deeds while on earth in his time of probation. This truth has been taught by various

Councils of the Church and popes since the 13th century. It is also included in the recent *Catechism of the Catholic Church*:

> 1022 Each man receives his eternal retribution in his immortal soul at the very moment of his death, *in a particular judgment* that refers his life to Christ: either entrance into the blessedness of heaven—through a purification or immediately—or immediate and everlasting damnation (emphasis added).

In the Middle Ages there was a debate about what happens to those who die before the Parousia or Second Coming of Christ at the end of the world. Basing herself on the words of Jesus in the Gospel and also on some statements of St. Paul, the Church gradually came to the conclusion that there is a *particular judgment* for each individual immediately after death. There is no explicit mention of this judgment in the New Testament, but the implication is there. This truth became part of the teaching of the Church and was incorporated into the Catechism since the 16th century. It is clearly taught in the *Catechism of the Council of Trent* (Part I, Article VII).

Accordingly, most of us learned in our catechism lessons that immediately after death the particular judgment takes place, in which the eternal fate of the deceased person is decided by Jesus, the Divine Judge. The expression "particular judgment" refers to the act of God by which the soul of man at death is either included among the number of the elect in heaven or is rejected by God for all eternity and suffers eternal damnation.

That there is a particular judgment of each person at the moment of death is not a defined dogma of the Catholic Church, but it is clearly implied in other dogmatic statements, so one can say that it is implicitly defined. For two ecumenical councils, the Second Council of Lyons in 1274 and the Council of Florence in 1439, declared that the souls of the just, free from all sin and after purification if they need it, are immediately assumed into heaven, and that the souls of those who die in mortal sin descend immediately into hell.

Likewise, Pope Benedict XII in the 14th century taught officially that the completely pure souls of the just, immediately after death or after their purgation, enter heaven and enjoy the immediate vision of God, while the souls of those who die in mortal sin descend immediately into hell.[1]

Sacred Scripture implies the existence of the particular judgment by teaching that immediately after death the departed souls receive their reward or punishment. The clearest and most frequently cited text is that of the parable of the rich man and Lazarus (Luke 16:19–31). There we learn that immediately after his death Lazarus is taken into the bosom of Abraham and the self-indulgent rich man, who has no concern for the poor, goes immediately to hell for punishment. There is no hesitation and no waiting for the end of the world. Another text that implies an immediate particular judgment concerns the good thief who died next to Christ on Calvary. To him Jesus said, "Truly, I say to you, today you will be with me in Paradise" (Luke 23:43).

For St. Paul death is the gateway to heaven and to personal communion with Christ: "My desire is to depart and be with Christ, for that is far better" (Phil. 1:23). Christ, of course, is already in heaven. These and similar texts gave rise, already in the second century, to the Christian reflection that some sort of judgment of each person takes place at the moment of death. Thus each deceased person learns immediately after death what his or her eternal destiny is. Thus all those who have died before us know exactly how they stand with God and what their eternal future will be—they do not have to wait for the general judgment at the end of the world in order to discover that.

It is fruitless to try to imagine what the particular judgment is like. We just cannot adequately picture these spiritual realities because all of our knowledge is based on and comes from the senses which are rooted in matter. The image of a judge and tribunal has been used in Christian art, and it does serve some useful purpose to make one think about the last things. But we should not think that such representations are accurate. The particular judgment involves a most intimate relation between the human person and the Divine Judge. There will, however, be no witnesses, cross-examination, accusers, defenders and so forth. For in a very true sense we have already judged ourselves, depending on how we have made use of God's abundant graces

---

1   *Benedictus Deus* (1336), D 1000–1001.

during this life. Our merits and sins go with us. We appear before God immediately at the moment of death bearing in our hands our good deeds and the record of our forgiven sins. Those who die in the state of mortal sin have already judged themselves; they have rejected God and God lets that rejection stand firm forever. Those who die in the state of sanctifying grace have chosen to believe in God and to serve him in this life. After death, adorned with grace and good works, they are admitted into the eternal kingdom of God as children and co-heirs with Christ. That is their particular judgment.

CHAPTER 6:
THOUGHTS ABOUT DEATH

The Imitation of Christ (Bk. I, Ch. 23)

The Imitation of Christ by Thomas à Kempis, written in the 15th century, has been a favorite book of spiritual reading for Catholics since at least the 16th century. Along with the New Testament, it was the most frequently read book by St. Ignatius Loyola, founder of the Society of Jesus which produced such saints as St. Francis Xavier, St. Peter Canisius and St. Robert Bellarmine, among many others. The thoughts contained in Chapter 23 of Book I are closely related to the material offered in the last chapter on the proper preparation for death. The key idea running through the Imitation is the well-known quote from the Bible:"Vanity of vanities, and all is vanity"—Ecclesiastes 1:2; the author completes it by adding "except to love God and serve him alone" (Book I, Ch. 1, 3). The English translation is reprinted here with permission from the Confraternity of the Precious Blood. The text has been altered slightly to be in accord with current English usage.

1. You must be gone from this world very quickly; reflect on how matters stand with you. Man is here today and gone tomorrow (1 Macc. 2:63).

And when he is out of sight he is also quickly out of mind.

O the dullness and hardness of man's heart, which thinks only of what is present, and looks not forward to things to come.

In every action and thought you should so order yourself as if you were immediately to die.

If you had a good conscience you would not much fear death.

It would be much better for you to fly from sin than to be afraid of death (Dan. 13:63)

If you are not prepared today, how will you be prepared

tomorrow? Tomorrow is an uncertain day. How do you know that you will be alive tomorrow? (James 4:13).

2. What benefit is there in living a long time when we advance so little in virtue?

Ah! Long life does not always make us better, but often adds to our guilt. Would to God we had behaved ourselves well in this world even for one day!

Many count the years of their conversion, but often the fruit of amendment is small.

If it is frightful to die, perhaps it will be more dangerous to live longer.

Blessed is he who has always the hour of death before his eyes and everyday is prepared to die (Sir. 7:36).

If you have ever seen a man die, remember that you also must go the same way.

3. In the morning consider that you will not live until evening; and when evening comes presume not that you will be alive the next morning.

Therefore, always be prepared, and live in such a way that death will never find you unprepared.

Many die suddenly and when they little expect it: "For the Son of Man is coming at an hour you do not expect" (Matt. 24:44).

When that last hour comes, you will begin to have quite different thoughts about your whole past life; and you will be very sorry that you have been so negligent and remiss.

4. How happy and prudent is the one who strives to be such now in this life as he desires to be found at death.

For it will give a man great confidence of dying happily if he has a perfect contempt of the world, a fervent desire of advancing in virtue, a love for discipline, the spirit of penance, a ready obedience, self-denial, and patience in bearing all adversities for the love of Christ.

You may do many good things when you are well, but when you are sick I do not know what you will be able to do.

Few are improved by sickness; they also that travel much abroad seldom become holy.

5. Trust not in your friends and relatives and do not put off the welfare of your soul to a later time; for men will sooner

forget you than you imagine. Don't forget: Out of sight, out of mind.

It is better now to provide for yourself while you have time, and to send some good before you, than to rely on the help of others after your death (Matt. 6:20).

If you are not now careful for yourself, who will be careful for you hereafter?

The present time is very precious: "Behold, now is the acceptable time; behold, now is the day of salvation" (2 Cor. 6:2).

But it is greatly to be lamented that you do not spend this time more profitably in which you may acquire the grace to live forever.

The time will come when you will wish for one day or one hour to amend your life, and I do not know whether you will obtain it.

6. O my dearly beloved, from how great a danger you can deliver yourself! From how great a fear you can be delivered, if you will right now be always fearful and expecting your death!

Strive now so to live that in the hour of your death you may rather rejoice than fear.

Learn now to die to the world that then you may begin to live with Christ (Rom. 6:8).

Learn now to despise all earthly things that then you may freely go to Christ.

Chastise your body now by penance that then you may have an assured confidence (1 Cor. 9:27).

7. Ah fool! Why do you think you will live long, when you are not sure of even one day? (Luke 12:20).

How many thinking to live long have been deceived and unexpectedly snatched away!

How often have you heard reported that this man was slain by the sword; another drowned; another falling from on high broke his neck; this man died at table; that other came to his end when he was at play.

Some have perished by fire; some by the sword; some by pestilence; some by robbers; and so death is the end of all, and man's life passes like a shadow (Eccles. 6:12).

8. Who will remember you when you are dead and who will pray for you?

Do now, beloved, do now all you can, because you do not know when you will die; nor do you know what will happen to you after death.

While you have time, acquire for yourself riches that will never die! (Matt. 6:20).

Think of nothing but your salvation—care for nothing but the things of God.

Now make friends for yourself by honoring the saints of God and imitating their lives that when you fail in this life they may receive you into their everlasting dwellings (Luke 16:9).

9. Keep yourself as a pilgrim and stranger on earth to whom the affairs of this world do not in the least belong (1 Pet. 2:11).

Keep your heart free and raised up towards God because you have not here a lasting city.

Send to God your daily prayers with sighs and tears that after death your spirit may be worthy to pass happily to our Lord. Amen.[1]

---

1   *My Imitation of Christ* by Thomas à Kempis, Revised Translation (Brooklyn, NY: Confraternity of the Precious Blood, 1954).

CHAPTER 7: THE DESIRE TO DIE

My desire is to depart and to be with Christ,
for that is far better. (Phil. 1:23)

Everything that exists strives for what is good for itself and so it strives to preserve itself in existence because existence is good. But there are times and situations in human life when death and an end to one's earthly existence seem to be a better option than remaining alive. Since man is a composed being that can come apart, he begins to die from the first moment of his existence. Death is absolutely certain for all living things on this earth; what remains hidden is the time of death. We all know that we will die, but we do not know the day or the hour. It is a good thing we do not know when we will die because, if we did know, it would cause constant worry and make life more difficult than it already is.

We read in the lives of the saints that many of them ardently desired to die and go to heaven. A good example of that is St. Ignatius of Antioch, the bishop condemned to death by the Romans. He pleaded with the Christians in Rome not to try to stop his martyrdom because he wanted to die as a victim of the hungry lions in the Coliseum so that he could be united with Christ.[1] St. John de Brebeuf, a North American Martyr in the 17ᵗʰ century, prayed that he would die a martyr at the hands of the Iroquois Indians. Given these facts, one may ask: Is it a morally good act to desire death as some of the saints did?

Man has a natural abhorrence of death because death means the loss of life and one's possessions. As the wise man said: "O death, how bitter is the reminder of you to one who

---

1   This request is made clear in the letter of St. Ignatius of to the Romans which was written about 107 A.D.

lives in peace among his possessions" (Sir. 41:1). Death separates one from relatives, friends and material possessions. That is why a man has a Last Will and Testament: before dying he assigns his remaining possessions, property and money, to relatives, friends and worthy causes. After death, he has no further use for them. Monks and nuns who have a vow of poverty do not confront this situation, since they do not own anything and therefore have nothing to leave to others. In a spiritual sense, when they take the vows of poverty, chastity and obedience they are dying to this world and anticipating their physical death some time in the future.

Human beings fear death for different reasons. Those who have a bad conscience loaded with many mortal sins, especially if they have lived a life of self-indulgence and have failed to pray and worship God, usually have an intense fear of death. That is a good thing for them, since it may move them to accept God's grace of repentance and seek reconciliation with God by having true sorrow for their sins and by making a good confession. Faithful Catholics who follow the Ten Commandments and pray regularly have less to fear because they are trying to do the will of God and so are friends of God and temples of the Holy Spirit. Those who are conformed to the divine will have a good conscience that assures them that they are pleasing to God and they are ready to expect the Lord when he comes. "Blessed are those servants whom the master finds awake when he comes" (Luke 12:37). In the parable of the Ten Virgins, it was the five wise virgins who were ready for the bridegroom and went in with him to the marriage feast, while the foolish ones were excluded (see Matt. 25:1–13).

We see, therefore, that sinners fear death, at least they should fear it if they have any understanding of what it means to be a creature of God and that they must give an accounting of their stewardship when they die. The just, however, even though they have a natural fear of death, can overcome the fear of death by the supernatural means of divine grace and the theological virtues of faith in Christ, hope and charity. Charity is especially important because it means the love of God and love seeks for union with the beloved. The more ardently one loves God the more he or she desires to be united with God.

Spiritual authors offer several reasons why it is lawful and morally good to desire to die. The first reason, which many sick and old people experience, is because they want to be liberated from a miserable life. This truth finds expression in the Bible: "Death is better than a miserable life, and eternal rest than chronic sickness" (Sir. 30:17). Christians who feel that way know from divine revelation that, if they make it to heaven, there will be no more pain or tears (Rev. 21:4). Because of the pains and difficulties of life God made it very short in comparison with eternity. The life of man on this earth is threescore and ten, and fourscore for those who are strong according to Psalm 90.

A second lawful reason for desiring death is to avoid the evils of the world and the persecution of the Church. In a situation of persecution by Ahab and his wife Jezebel, the prophet Elijah prayed for death (1 Kings 19:4). Also Judas Maccabeus said, "It is better for us to die in battle than to see the misfortunes of our nation and of the sanctuary" (1 Macc. 3:59).

A third reason is to avoid being in a state of life where one can offend God by sin. In this life man is free to choose: it is a time of trial and probation to make oneself worthy of heaven by practicing the virtues of faith, hope and charity. Here we are subject to serious temptations from the world, the flesh and the devil. In this regard the dead are better off than the living, at least those who are saved either in heaven or in purgatory, because they are no longer able to commit sin. The saved are confirmed in goodness and the love of God for all eternity and they cannot change. It is not just a matter of avoiding mortal sin. Sin is the greatest evil in the world; a serious Christian will do all he can to avoid deliberate venial sins and even minor imperfections. We are all weak, burdened with concupiscence and prone to evil, for as the wise man said, "a righteous man falls seven times" (Prov. 24:16). One may lawfully desire to die in order to be freed from this possibility of sin.

The above are valid reasons for wishing to die, but the best reason is to leave this temporal life in order to be with Christ in heaven forever. St. Paul is a prime example of a man who desired to die and be with Christ as he wrote in Phil. 1:23, "My desire is to depart and to be with Christ." Paul did not desire death in order to escape trials and sufferings; he said he "rejoiced" in his sufferings (Rom. 5:3). He wanted to die and be with Christ because of his intense love for him: "Neither death nor life… nor anything else in all creation will be able to separate us from the love of God in Christ Jesus our Lord" (Rom. 8:38–39). The same can be said of many saints and martyrs like St. Ignatius of Antioch, St. Francis of Assisi, St. Stanislaus Kostka and St. Maximilian Kolbe.

Spiritual writers like St. Bernard and St. Ignatius Loyola said that there are three degrees of humility or love for the Christian in his relation to God. The first degree is to keep the Commandments and avoid all mortal sin. The person in this degree would not commit a mortal sin for the whole world. The second degree is the life of the counsels which means striving for perfection and avoiding all deliberate venial sins. The third and highest degree is love for Jesus Christ and the desire to imitate him in all things; to suffer reproach and rejection as he did; they desire to be dissolved and to be with him. Those in this state accept the limitations of this life as the will of God but earnestly desire to be freed from it and to be united with Christ forever for, as St. Paul said, "[T]hat is far better" (Phil. 1:23).

CHAPTER 8:
DEATH AND ETERNITY

*This is eternal life, that they know thee, the only true God,
and Jesus Christ whom thou hast sent. (John 17:3)*

Man is totally immersed in the world of time and space. Everything we know has a beginning, middle and end. We think in terms of minutes, hours, days and years. That is characteristic of bodies in motion. Time is defined as the measure of motion of before and after. It is a type of existence that has succession of one moment after another. The present moment, now, is between the past and the future, but the "now" is constantly changing or moving.

Eternity is a type of existence in which there is no movement, no succession, no beginning and no end. Only God is eternal in the full sense of the word, because only God is totally immutable and the fullness of being with no beginning and no end. The classic definition of eternity was formulated by Boethius in the 5th century. He said that eternity is the absolutely perfect and simultaneous possession of interminable life. Since God is his own being he is eternity. The three Persons in the Trinity are called eternal by St. Athanasius in his famous profession of faith called "Quicumque": "The Father is eternal, the Son is eternal, and the Holy Spirit is eternal. Nevertheless, there are not three eternal beings, but one eternal being."[1] We have no direct knowledge of eternity because all of our knowledge comes through our five senses and they perceive only bodies in motion. We do not know spiritual realities directly; we arrive at them by reason and by negation, that is, we remove from them the limitations of bodies in motion such as we are. We can do

---

1   D 75; see also St. Thomas Aquinas, STh I, 10, 1.

that because our thinking, our ideas are spiritual and are not limited to time and space. Our body is in the "now," but with our mind we can transcend that and think of the past which no longer exists, and the future which does not yet exist.

Spiritual creatures like angels and the human soul are naturally immortal because they are not composed of parts the way bodies are. Plants and animals die after some time because they are composed of parts and eventually those parts are separated. That is what we mean by death. Angels and human souls have a beginning, since they are created by God, but they have no end because they have no parts and so are not subject to corruption. That is why we say that they are immortal. When human beings die the soul continues to live in a different way. Those who are saved enter into unending life with God which the Bible refers to as eternal or everlasting life; those who are lost go to hell and are condemned to eternal death and punishment. St. Thomas Aquinas says that they "participate" in the eternity of God because they will live forever, but they did have a beginning since they were created, whereas God has no beginning and no end.

Since we are limited by time and space it is difficult for us to think in terms of eternity. At times perhaps we get a taste of it when we are very happy and enjoying the company of those we love. We spend hours with friends without being aware of the passage of time and are surprised to learn how late it is. When we are happy in that way, we say that "time flies." Eternal life must be something like that. We arrive at some idea of eternity as a type of duration by denying of it the limitations of time that we are familiar with.

In the Bible there is a very close connection between life and eternity, and death and eternity. Both ideas are mentioned many times, especially by the Lord Jesus in the New Testament. In the Old Testament it occurs in the Psalms and in the wisdom literature—Proverbs, Ecclesiastes, Sirach and Wisdom. In the Gospels our Lord mentions eternal life many times; he mentions hell and eternal damnation more than thirty times.

Regarding the eternity of God himself we read in Psalm 90:4, "In your sight a thousand years are as the passing of one day or as a watch in the night." In Psalm 102 we pray, "But thou,

O Lord, art enthroned forever; thy name endures to all generations" (v. 12), and "[B]ut thou art the same, and thy years have no end" (v. 27). We noted that "lack of succession" is essential to eternity. That this is characteristic of God is found in Jesus' striking words: "I tell you most solemnly, before Abraham ever was, I AM" (John 8:58).

Eternal life is often mentioned by Jesus and it is identified with knowing God and Jesus: "This is eternal life: to know you the only true God, and Jesus Christ whom you have sent" (John 17:3). John 3:16 is a well known quote that one sees at times at football games or on signs in front of a house: "God so loved the world that he gave his only Son, that everyone who has faith in him may not perish but have eternal life." Again, after Jesus' sermon on the bread of life, when some disciples left him because they would not accept it, Peter, when asked if he would also leave, said to Jesus: "Lord, to whom shall we go? You have the words of eternal life" (John 6:68).

The idea of eternity in the Bible is also applied to sinners who die as enemies of God—their lot is also eternal. In the parable of the sheep and the goats in Matthew 25, the king says at the conclusion regarding the good and the bad: "And they will go away to eternal punishment, but the righteous will enter eternal life (Matt 25:46).

The above is just a sampling of the many references to eternity in the Bible. The Church teaches us that God is eternal. We also find it in the liturgy in the various creeds composed down through the centuries. In the Apostles' Creed we pray: "I believe in the resurrection of the body and life everlasting." At Mass on Sunday in the Nicene Creed we pray: "I believe...in the life of the world to come."

It is a sobering thought to think that, when I die—and it can happen any day when we least expect it—I will live forever either in heaven with God or in hell separated from him. I will be in eternity. Since time ends and eternity does not, eternity is more important for me than time. St. Augustine said, "What is not eternal, is nothing." Think about that. God made me immortal and this means that I have an eternal destiny either in heaven or in hell, depending on how I live my life either with God or against him. There is no other alternative. Annihilation, a possibility, will not happen because when God does something he does not change his mind. Since he created angels and men immortal they will remain immortal for all eternity. So I am destined for either eternal happiness or eternal misery, depending on how I respond to God's love and mercy.

Since we live in a secular and materialistic culture, now strongly influenced by atheism, spiritual realities are ignored and often denied, especially revealed truths about eternity, personal survival after death, the devil and hell. It is a curious phenomenon that many of our contemporaries, who do not believe in the reality of hell, often use the word "hell" in daily conversation. Moreover, a common assumption in our culture now, either implicit or explicit, is that man's life totally ends with death of the body. And many of those who say that they believe in the future life seem to assume that everyone goes to heaven. Most Americans seem to believe in heaven, but very few seem to believe in hell.

A few years ago I read an essay about the nature of sporting events and why it is that so many people enjoy going to big sporting events like football, soccer, baseball, basketball, auto racing and so forth. The author said he thinks many people go to such games that absorb their complete attention so that they can forget about the inevitability of death. Of course this desire is not stated explicitly, but the author thinks it is present implicitly. To what extent that is true, I do not know, but that it applies to many is probably true.

Catholics who believe in the divinity of Jesus Christ and believe what he said about the nature of God and about man should take the teaching of the Church about eternal life very seriously. Life is not a game that can be played and then forgotten. Life is a deadly serious business, especially when you realize that you will live forever—either happily with God or miserably without him. Since I am a limited creature, I had a beginning in my mother's womb when God created me. I had a beginning, but there is no end to my life as a human person. Death of the body, which comes to all of us, means entrance of my soul, my person and my self-consciousness of who I am, into eternity with God, the angels and the saints. At Jesus' Second Coming at the end of the world, my soul will be reunited to my body and I will rise from the dead to live forever—either in heaven or in hell. That being the case, St. Paul tells us that now is the time of salvation; now is the time to grow in the knowledge and love of God. Now is the time to work out my salvation in fear and trembling as he did (see Phil. 2:12).

In order to reach heaven and to gain eternal life I must live the way God designed me to live. Since he made me free, I am free to follow his law or to reject it. To live as I should means having faith in Jesus Christ as my Savior, receiving the Sacraments of the Church, praying daily, practicing self-restraint and controlling evil desires, trying to live according to God's law, and practicing love of God and neighbor which Jesus said is a summary of the whole law of God. So basically it means seeking the will of God in all things and living my life according to his rules, since he knows what is best for me, and not according to the rule of any modern philosophy or ideology.

Thoughts about death, eternity and eternal life are very sobering. It is spiritually healthy to meditate on eternity and to give thought to my eternal future. My life now on this earth, at this time and in this century, is a time of preparation for my eternal life. Out of his infinite love God made me free and he invites me to love him in return, but he will not force me to love him or to live according to his rules. Human freedom is a great gift from God, but it is also quite mysterious. God gives most of us 70 or 80 years to work out our salvation, to reach maturity in our knowledge and love of God and to work out our salvation. His grace is always there to help me, but he respects my freedom. So my eternal future is in my hands.

Human life is a great adventure—the greatest of all adventures because it has eternal consequences. My death signals the beginning of those consequences. These reflections on eternity—eternal life or eternal misery—are meant to help you put order into your life and to motivate you to live the way God wants you to live so that you can attain the end he planned for you—eternal happiness that you can never lose and that no one can take away from you.

CHAPTER 9: AFTER DEATH

No eye has seen, nor ear heard, nor the heart of man conceived,
what God has prepared for those who love him. (1 Cor. 2:9)

The conclusion of the last chapter made the point that life has consequences—eternal consequences for us after we die and leave this world of time and space. The wise person is the one who plans for the future and prepares for his future. God gives us a limited amount of time to prepare ourselves for the next life because we do not have here a lasting city or home. Our eternal future in heaven or hell depends on how we conduct ourselves in this life.

It is important to realize that we do not live in a purely natural order. The reason is that God raised us to the supernatural level; he became man in Jesus Christ and offers us, through his grace, the reward of the face to face vision of God for all eternity if we do his will and abide by his law. Our nature in itself does not demand the face to face vision of God. It is a gift given to us by God over and above the demands of our nature. That is why it is called "super-natural," that is, our nature as such does not require the Beatific Vision of God. It is a loving gift of God that goes beyond nature.

Our eternal future, therefore, depends on the state of our soul at the moment of death. Sinners go to hell and the just, those in the state of sanctifying grace, go to heaven—immediately if worthy, and after some purification if they are not ready for heaven. This raises the question of what the Church means by sin and what she means by grace.

Sin and Damnation

In reality, sin is a deadly serious matter. In our secular culture sin is not taken seriously because God is not taken seriously by many of our contemporaries. One company has gone so far as to name one of its perfumes for women "My Sin." Apparently, whoever came up with that thinks that sin is something positive and attractive. Here we are reflecting on the mystery of death. We have already seen that sin—the sin of Adam and Eve at the beginning—is the cause of death. If Adam had not sinned, there would be no death in the world. Sin is possible in this world because man is free to obey God or to disobey him. Sin in all its various forms means to freely choose and prefer some creature in place of the Creator. Pride, preferring oneself to God, is involved in every sin. Man can choose sin but "the wages of sin is death" as St. Paul stated it clearly (Rom. 6:23).

St. Augustine said that sin is any thought, word or deed contrary to the law of God. Man knows instinctively the natural law which tells him in his conscience to do good and to avoid evil. In the practical order this comes down to doing what is reasonable and respecting the rights of others. All this is basically expressed in the Ten Commandments, which can be summarized by love of God and love of neighbor as oneself. Another way of putting it is to say that sin is aversion from God and conversion towards creatures.

The causes of sin are both internal and external. The internal causes are ignorance, concupiscence and malice because of a distorted will. The external causes of sin are the world and the devil. Because of Adam's Original Sin we also inherit "concupiscence" which is a tendency towards rebellion against God, and love of self to the point of violating the rights of others.

There are two aspects of sin: guilt and punishment. There is guilt because of the offense against God the Creator. The guilt of sin can be removed by repentance and asking God for forgiveness, especially in the Sacrament of Penance. But there is also punishment associated with sin. The Church calls it "the temporal punishment due to sin." This can be taken away by penance in this life (prayer, fasting and almsgiving), or by suffering in purgatory after one dies in the state of grace.

There are two kinds of sin that are essentially different: Mortal sin and venial sin. Mortal sin is a serious offense against God. The mortal sinner loses sanctifying grace which makes one a child of God and heir of heaven. He separates himself from

God. If the sinner dies in this state, he goes directly to hell for-ever. The Church teaches that, in order to commit a mortal sin, there must be *serious matter* (murder, adultery, blasphemy, etc), *sufficient reflection* of what one is doing, that is, one must know that it is evil and forbidden by God, and *full consent of the will.* If one of these is lacking, the act will be a venial sin.

Venial sin is any offense against God which is less than a mortal sin, such as telling a lie of convenience, speaking unchar-itably about others, impatience, eating too much, gossiping, and so forth. Venial sins lessen one's love of God and, if deliberate, can lead one gradually into mortal sin. Venial sins do not de-stroy sanctifying grace, but they diminish it.

Jesus came into this world to save us from our sins and to make it possible for us to attain perfect happiness in heaven. The important and decisive role of sin in the history of mankind is clearly expressed by the words Jesus himself used at the Last Sup-per when he changed wine into his blood—words that are re-peated at every celebration of the Mass: THIS IS THE CUP OF MY BLOOD, THE BLOOD OF THE NEW AND EVERLASTING COVENANT...THIS BLOOD WILL BE SHED FOR YOU AND FOR MANY *SO THAT SINS MAY BE FORGIVEN* (see Matt. 26:28).

The New Testament says many times that the reason for the Incarnation of God was and is to save men from their sins. Jesus Christ is the Messiah promised in the Old Testament and in He-brew the very name "Jesus" means "savior." Savior from what? Savior from sin and the consequences of sin. In the very first chapter of the New Testament, the angel said to Joseph: "Joseph, son of David, do not fear to take Mary as your wife....she will bear a son, and you shall call his name Jesus, for he will save his people from their sins (Matt. 1:21). Sin, therefore, must be extremely important because, in order to save men from their sins, the Lord God Almighty himself, Creator of heaven and earth, became man and intervened in human history by his In-carnation *"so that sins may be forgiven."*

Grace and Merit

The idea of "grace," both actual and sanctifying, is very common in Catholic theology, spirituality and catechetics. Sanctifying grace is defined as the supernatural life of the soul that makes us children of God and heirs of heaven. Grace is a special gift from God, communicated to us by faith in God, Baptism and the other sacraments, that elevates the soul to a new level. It is something like a new birth that makes it possible for us to enter heaven and to see God face to face (see John 3:5). In a mysterious way, grace is a sharing in the divine life of God. St. Peter said that it even makes us participate in the divine life (2 Pet. 1:4). The reception of God's grace is often called sanctification or justification. Grace is a spiritual quality that inheres in the soul and transforms it and elevates it to the supernatural level.

Adam and Eve lost sanctifying grace for themselves and their descendants by their sin. It was restored to us by Jesus through his passion, death and resurrection. In order to save one's soul and enter into heaven after death, it is absolutely necessary to die possessing divine grace, the life of the soul. In the working out of the salvation of each human person God helps man not merely by the interior principle of divine grace, but also by exterior actual graces, such as the life of Christ, revelation of God's will in the Bible, the teaching of the Church and the reception of the sacraments. The ultimate goal of grace is the Beatific Vision of God for all eternity.

According to the Bible, grace is the condescension or special benevolence and favor shown by God to human beings. In the objective sense, grace is the unmerited gift that proceeds from this benevolent disposition. In the thinking of the Church, grace is something more than the gifts of nature, such as creation and the gift of life. Grace is a supernatural gift of God that he bestows freely on rational creatures so that they can attain personal union with him. Grace, by communicating divine life to the soul, makes it possible for a man to become a child of God. And because of our divine sonship, we are able to call God "our Father." An essential aspect of grace is its gratuity, since by his nature man has no claim or right to it. It is a pure gift because God is love and he wills to communicate his own life and goodness to human persons.[1]

---

1   This presentation of grace is based on my *Fundamentals of Catholicism*, Vol. 3 (San Francisco: Ignatius Press, 1983), 13–28.

Closely related to the idea of grace is the idea of "merit." Merit is a common idea in Catholic theology and spirituality; it was denied and rejected by Luther and the other Protestant reformers. Catholics often speak about meriting an increase of grace or meriting heaven. As understood in Catholic theology, merit means a work performed for the benefit of another, on whom it establishes a claim for a reward. So merit and reward are correlative terms. The woman who goes out of her way to help someone in difficulty deserves a reward of some kind.

Merit therefore is related to justice which means giving to each person what is due to him. The Catholic teaching about merit comes to this: the person in the state of sanctifying grace who performs good works of any kind out of love for God will merit a reward for it from God. In order to earn rewards in heaven the person performing a good work must be in the state of grace. The Council of Trent in the 16th century taught that, for the justified person, eternal life is both a grace promised by God and a reward for his own good works and merits.[2] The Council points out that God's grace is required to perform any and all good works; in his goodness God makes these good works (which depend on his grace) also meritorious of further grace and eternal life.

With regard to merit, Jesus promises rich rewards to those who, for his sake, suffer persecution: "Be glad and rejoice for your reward is very great in heaven" (Matt. 5:12). At the end of the world Jesus, the Divine Judge, will decree eternal reward for the just on the basis of their merits and good works: "Come, O blessed of my Father, inherit the kingdom prepared for you from the foundation of the world; for I was hungry and you gave me food…" (Matt. 25:34ff.). St. Paul teaches that each one's reward is proportioned to the good works performed: "For he will render to every man according to his works" (Rom. 2:6).

When St. Paul refers to his own eternal reward as "a crown of justice which the Lord, the just Judge, will give to me in that day" (2 Tim. 4:8), he shows that the good works of the just establish a claim on God for a reward. So grace gives man the power to perform works that deserve a reward from God. That is what we mean by merit.

2   D 1545–1550.

In the context of our reflections on the mystery of death, the grace that we accumulate in this life, along with the reward we merit because of our good works—prayer, penance, almsgiving, attendance at Mass and receiving the other Sacraments—determine our place in heaven and the level of our happiness there for all eternity. After one dies there is no possibility of merit and increased rewards. Therefore it is important for our eternal future that we strive now, while we have the time, to grow daily in the grace of God and to perform good works that will merit for us a high place in heaven. Just as the closer you are to a fire the warmer it is, so also, the closer you are to God the more you enjoy his goodness and beauty. This means that there are various degrees of happiness in heaven. In short, the more grace and merits you have acquired in this life, the greater will be your happiness in heaven. Merit is like having a heavenly savings account: if you add to it each day by virtuous living and good works, when you die you will get a substantial reward from God. That being the case, the wise Christian will avoid all deliberate sin and try to love God and neighbor by leading a virtuous life. What we do now in time determines what we shall be in the eyes of God for all eternity.[3]

When I die, will I go to purgatory?

Young people do not think much about death because they are strong and death is remote. Old people think about death often, perhaps every day. A famous psychiatrist wrote that all of his patients over the age of 35 were concerned about death and what would happen to them after they died. From the Bible and the teaching of the Church we know for certain that our soul after death faces three possibilities: 1) purgatory; 2) heaven; 3) hell. Those who go to purgatory have sanctifying grace and so are saved, but before going to heaven they must make satisfaction for sins committed that have not yet been atoned for. There is only one exit from purgatory and that is to heaven. The two eternal futures for those who die is either heaven or hell.

3   On the theology of merit see: *Fundamentals of Catholicism,* Vol. 3, 77–86.

Since Vatican II in Sunday homilies and in catechism classes there has not been much mention of purgatory and the need to offer Masses and prayers for the souls of relatives and friends who have died. Many Catholics do not know about purgatory or take it seriously and so, when a relative or friend dies, they do not pray for them or offer Masses for them. Too often at funerals the impression is given that the deceased person is already in heaven. Maybe yes, maybe no. In any event, the Church urges us to pray for the dead in case they need our help to get out of purgatory.

Purgatory is an exercise of the justice of God who is infinitely merciful but also infinitely just and holy. Because of God's holiness no one can enter into his presence in heaven unless he is totally clean, pure and holy—only saints can enter there. This means that those who die in the state of sanctifying grace, if they still have venial sins on their soul and if they have not made complete satisfaction for sins committed during life, must be cleansed and purified before they can be admitted to heaven. That takes place in purgatory.

There is no doubt about the existence of purgatory because it is an infallible dogma and teaching of the Catholic Church. Purgatory is the place or condition in which the souls of the just are purified after death to prepare them for entry into heaven.

Private revelations tell us that even very holy persons, including nuns and monks, spend some time in purgatory before going to heaven. This is for their minor faults and imperfections. If that is the case with holy nuns and monks, then how foolish it is for us to think that a relative, who perhaps committed serious sins in the past, goes directly to heaven. A practical consequence of the truth about purgatory is that we should always offer Masses and prayers for loved ones who have died in order to help them and hasten their entrance into heaven. That is an act of charity and love for our neighbor.

The nature of the purification in purgatory has not been revealed to us. Theologians speculate about it, but we do not have certain knowledge. In Scripture and the writing of the Fathers of the Church it is referred to as "fire" or something like fire. The Church does not teach that it is a "physical fire," even though preachers and theologians may speak about "the fires of purgatory." The official declarations of the Councils of the Church speak only of "purifying punishments," not of purifying fire. Whatever it is, it is painful and causes suffering. St. Thomas Aquinas said that one hour in purgatory involves more suffering than many years of intense suffering on earth. Think about that!

Since the punishment in purgatory is proportioned to the debt to be paid, the suffering is not the same for all. Therefore the length of time in purgatory depends on the size of the debt to be paid and the seriousness of the forgiven sins one has committed.

Through the constant practice of the Church, manifested clearly in her liturgy, we know that the sufferings of the souls in purgatory can be alleviated and totally removed by the Masses, prayers and penances of faithful Christians on earth. This truth is intimately related to the "communion of saints" and the Mystical Body of Christ. The faithful on earth, in purgatory and in heaven form one Church in different stages. The souls in purgatory cannot merit and so cannot help themselves, but we can help them by our prayers and by gaining indulgences for them. That is why we should constantly pray for the souls in purgatory.

There is no hope in hell because the damned are lost forever. There is no hope in heaven because the saved have reached their final goal. But there is lots of hope in purgatory because the souls there know they are saved and will eventually get to heaven. Therefore in spite of their suffering there is great joy in purgatory. That being the case, they willingly and joyfully suffer for their past sins while they wait to be released into the eternal happiness of heaven.[4]

The Particular Judgment

Any person who reflects on his mortality must wonder what will happen to him when he dies. Basing herself on the words of Jesus in the Gospel and also on statements of St. Paul, the Church gradually came to the conclusion that there is a

4   *Ibid.*, 373–376.

"particular judgment" for each person immediately after death when the soul leaves the body. The teaching about this can be found in the *Catechism of the Catholic Church* sec. 1021–1022.

The phrase "particular judgment" refers to that act of God by which the soul of man at death is either saved or lost and the person knows what his destiny is. The teaching of the Church is directed against certain errors of those who claimed that the souls of the dead are held in some type of suspended animation or a perpetual "sleep" until the end of the world and the Second Coming of Christ to judge the living and the dead. Denying that those who die in Christ attain the Beatific Vision right now, those holding this view said that the dead are not judged until the final general judgment. Church teaching on the particular judgment has already been treated in detail above in Chapter 5.

Damnation and Hell

Since the human soul is immortal, it will live on forever after death and separation from the body. From divine revelation we know with certainty that there are two possible states for the soul after death—happiness with God in heaven or misery with Satan in hell. Those are the only two possibilities. There is no such thing as annihilation or simply ceasing to exist as is the case with the souls of dogs, horses, fish and all brute animals. The reason for this is that man's soul is *spiritual* by nature; this means that it has no parts and so cannot lose existence as plants and animals can.

It is spiritually helpful to think seriously about the reality of hell. The more one thinks about it the more terrifying it is. Since man is a social being, for happiness he needs the loving friendship and association with others. In hell there is none of that. There is no love there but only hate and misery. The damned in hell are rejected, isolated and alone; they suffer and there is no one to love or comfort them. There is no hope in hell because the sinners there rejected God and so God lets that stand, since he will not force any person to love him. In addition, there is the positive punishment of the damned. We do not know exactly what it is, but the Bible speaks of it as the "fires" of hell; Our Lord says several times that the damned are cast into the outer darkness where there is weeping and gnashing of teeth (Matt. 8:12; 13:42; 22:13; 24:51; 25:30; Luke 13:28).

As mentioned before, it is a curious fact that many people use the word "hell" frequently in their daily conversation, but do not believe in hell. If they really believed in hell and that they could go there after they die, they would not be so flippant in the use of the word.

Hell is defined as the place and state of eternal punishment for the fallen angels and the human beings who die in the state of unrepented mortal sin. The existence of hell is a defined and infallible doctrine of the Catholic Church. Anyone who denies the existence of hell rejects the clear teaching of the Church and the clear teaching of divine revelation of the Lord Jesus in the Bible.

Here are a few of the proofs for the existence of hell. The 5th century Athanasian Creed states that, when Christ comes in glory at the end of the world, all will have to give an accounting of their life and "those who have done good deeds will go into eternal life; those who have done evil will go into everlasting fire."[5]

Pope Benedict XII declared in 1336 (*Benedictus Deus*): "We define that, according to the general decree of God, the souls of those who die in actual mortal sin go down into hell soon after their death, and there suffer the pains of hell."[6]

The teaching of the Church about hell is based on the Bible and divine revelation. The New Testament mentions hell more than thirty times. Jesus often threatens sinners with the punishment of hell, if they do not repent. For example, he calls it "eternal fire" (Matt. 18:8), "the hell of fire" (Matt. 18:9), "unquenchable fire" (Mark 9:43). St. Paul says of sinners that "They shall suffer the punishment of eternal destruction and exclusion from the presence of the Lord and from the glory of his might" (2 Thess. 1:9).

Catholic theology distinguishes a twofold punishment in hell: *the pain of loss* and *the pain of sense*. The pain of loss, which

5   D 76.
6   D 1002.

is the essence of damnation and the most important, consists in exclusion from the Beatific Vision and rejection by God. This is indicated by those fearful words of Jesus, the Eternal Judge: "Depart from me, you cursed, into the eternal fire prepared for the devil and his angels" (Matt. 25:41).

The pain of sense consists in the suffering which is caused by external agents because the damned will suffer also in their body after the resurrection and the Last Judgment. The Bible describes hell vividly as a place where there is weeping and gnashing of teeth, a place of sorrow, intense suffering and despair.

It is clear from the repeated warnings of Jesus in the Gospels that the duration of punishment in hell is eternal. On this point the Fourth Lateran Council in 1215 A.D. declared that the wicked "will receive perpetual punishment with the devil."[7] The word "eternal" should not be understood in the sense of "a very long time, but finally coming to an end," since there is an obvious parallel between eternal punishment and eternal life in the parable in Matthew 25. Just as heaven will never end, so also hell will never end. The interpretation of Origen in the 3rd century that the devils and sinners in hell, after a long period of suffering, will all eventually get to heaven, has been condemned by the Church several times.

There is a correlation between the existence of hell and divine justice. The damned angels and human beings give witness to the justice of God because he respects personal freedom, and those who are lost have really condemned themselves by rejecting God's abundant grace. The damned cannot repent because their will is hardened in evil and hatred of God; in such a state they cannot repent.

Those in hell do not all suffer the same punishment. It is the common opinion of theologians that their punishment is proportioned to each one's guilt. The Second Council of Lyons in 1274 defined as Catholic teaching that "the souls of those who die in mortal sin...soon go down into hell, but *there they receive different punishments.*"[8]

7   D 801.
8   D 858.

Hell, like death, is an unpleasant subject to talk about because it is an unpleasant reality. But eternal damnation in hell is a possibility for each one of us after death if we do not keep God's commandments and practice love of God and neighbor. In the Gospels Jesus, who knows all things, has given us sufficient warning. Remember what he said about Judas who betrayed him and then committed suicide: "It would have been better for that man if he had not been born" (Matt. 26:24; Mark 14:21). Many saints and theologians have taken that to mean that Judas is in hell. Thoughts about hell keep us humble and help us to avoid all mortal sin. Reflect on what the author of *The Imitation of Christ* wrote in Book I, Chapter 23: "If the love of God cannot restrain you from evil, then at least let the fear of hell restrain you."[9]

Happiness in Heaven

Every human person seeks happiness, and would like to make it permanent with the avoidance of suffering, but that is not possible in this life because of human mortality and mutability, and because of the consequent trials and disappointments that one encounters every day. And if one does achieve a certain level of happiness, it is never permanent because death, either sudden or after a long life, separates us from life on this planet, from our friends and possessions. Limited human happiness is fragile, temporary and can easily be lost. Man seeks permanent, perfect happiness, but he cannot find it in this life. Does this mean that man will always be frustrated? By no means.

The Christian answer to this problem is the promise of Jesus of eternal life with God in heaven for those who believe in him and do his will. The source of life and happiness is God our Creator who is infinite being, life and goodness. He wants to share his abundant life with those who do his will, love him and die with his grace. Perfect, permanent happiness cannot be found in this life, but it is promised to those who die as friends of God. Those who have achieved that are in "heaven."

9   For more on the above about hell see *Fundamentals of Catholicism*, Vol. 3, 370–373.

Heaven is the place and condition of perfect, supernatural happiness with God and all the saints. Heaven, like death and hell, is very mysterious to us. St. Paul stresses the mysterious nature of heaven when he says: "No eye has seen, nor ear heard, nor the heart of man conceived, what God has prepared for those who love him" (1 Cor. 2:9). From these words of Paul it is clear that love is an essential part of heaven because God himself is love (1 John 4:16).

What the Church teaches about heaven is very consoling and fills us with hope. She says that the souls of the saved who at the moment of death are free from all guilt of sin and free from the punishment due to sin in purgatory, go immediately to heaven. We profess our belief in this revealed truth every time we pray the Apostles' Creed: "I believe...in life everlasting," and when we pray the Creed at Sunday Mass: "We look for the resurrection of the dead, the life of the world to come."

In the Gospels Jesus speaks clearly and often about heaven. In the Gospels we find many parables about the "kingdom of heaven" and the "kingdom of God." Jesus vividly paints the happiness of heaven in the image of a wedding feast (see Matt. 25:10) and calls it eternal life. The knowledge of God and of Christ is itself eternal life: "This is eternal life, that they know thee the only true God, and Jesus Christ whom thou hast sent" (John 17:3).

St. John the Apostle stresses in his writings that one attains eternal life and heaven by believing in Jesus, the Messiah and Son of God (see John 3:16; 20:31; 1 John 5:13). He also says that heaven consists in conformity to God and in the direct vision of God: "We know that when he appears we shall be like him, for we shall see him as he is" (1 John 3:2). Please note that the idea of life is always associated with heaven; so life and heaven go together. Heaven is abundant life that will never end and that no one can ever take away from those who possess it.

The basic human acts that constitute heavenly happiness are the knowledge and love of God and joy or the fulfillment of all man's desires. Heaven does not consist in eating, drinking, possessions and sexual activity. Many people wonder about whether or not they will know their parents, relatives, spouse, children and friends in heaven. On this point many Catholic theologians have taught that the blessed in heaven, in addition to the vision of God, also enjoy the companionship of their loved ones and all the saints.

Another question often asked is whether or not all the saved are equal in the sense that they have the same degree of enjoyment of the Beatific Vision? In other words, are some more happy than others? It is a great grace to save one's soul and get to heaven, but it is the infallible teaching of the Catholic Church that the level of participation in the Beatific Vision granted to the saved is proportioned to each one's merits. In the 15th century the Council of Florence defined that the saved "see clearly the Triune God himself, just as he is, *some more perfectly than others* according to their respective merits."[10] Accordingly, Jesus promised that he will "repay every man for what he has done" (Matt. 16:27). On the same point St. Paul said that "each shall receive his wages according to his labor" (1 Cor. 3:8). Also, Jesus words about "many rooms" in his Father's house have often been interpreted, in Catholic tradition, as affirming the inequality of rewards, depending on each one's merits (see John 14:2). However, it should be remembered that, although there are different degrees of happiness, all those in heaven are perfectly happy in accordance with their capacity for joy.

There is, therefore, a direct and close connection between death and heaven. Now our life is short and full of trials and tribulations. If we keep his commandments and try to do his will, if we pray daily and receive the sacraments, we have moral certitude that, when we die, which we surely will sooner or later, we will go to heaven and enjoy eternal life and a perfect happiness that no one can take away from us.

The Resurrection of the Dead

We have reflected on the particular judgment, purgatory, hell and heaven as what will happen to each one of us when we die. But there is more. Jesus has revealed to us that history as we know it at some time in the future will come to an end. History and time will stop at the Second Coming of Christ at the end of

10   D 1305.

the world; that will be accompanied by the resurrection of the dead in preparation for the General Judgment of all mankind from Adam to his last descendant. These glorious truths are expressed in the Creed when we pray: "He will come again in glory to judge the living and the dead and his kingdom will have no end." Now we will consider the resurrection of the dead.

It is a defined and infallible truth of the Catholic faith, based on the revelation of Jesus Christ, that all mankind, both good and evil, will rise from the dead at the end of the world, in imitation of Jesus who rose from the dead three days after he was crucified and died. The word "resurrection" means the return to life in the body of a dead human being. Resurrection at the end of the world will not be like the resurrection of Lazarus and others recounted in the Bible who eventually died and were buried. Resurrection in Christ at the end of the world means taking on a completely new type of existence. It means that the souls of all those who have died will be reunited to their bodies and will remain united to them forever.

In the Gospels Jesus speaks clearly and often about the final resurrection of the body. He teaches not only the resurrection of the just (Luke 14:14), but also the resurrection of the wicked who will be cast into hell with their bodies (Matt. 5:29–30). In his words to Martha Jesus actually identifies himself with the resurrection of the body: "I am the resurrection and the life" (John 11:25). In John 6 he promises resurrection on the last day to those who believe in him and partake of the Eucharist.

Belief in the resurrection as proclaimed by Jesus was an essential and major part of the early preaching of the Church. It occupies a large part in Peter's first sermon on Pentecost (Acts 2); it is an essential part of the good news of salvation in Jesus Christ preached by Peter, Paul and the other Apostles (see Acts 3, 4, 5, 10, 17, 24, 26). The resurrection of the dead will take place at the end of the world at a time known only to the Father (Mark 13:32; Acts 1:7).

According to Catholic teaching the dead will rise again with the same bodies they had on earth. It implicitly affirms this when it speaks of the resurrection or "re-awakening" of the body. St. Paul says in 1 Cor. 15:53, "For this perishable nature must put on the imperishable, and this mortal nature must put on immortality." Addressing the same point, the Fourth Lateran Council in 1215 declared: "And all these will rise *with their own bodies which they now have* so that they may receive according to their works...."[11]

When the Church says "with their own bodies" she does not mean they will have the exact same physical elements, since the matter in our bodies changes about every five years. What it means is that our soul will inform matter in such a way that we will look the same, as a mature person, and will retain our sexual differentiation as either a man or a woman.

It is a common opinion among theologians that both the saved and the damned will rise again from the dead. The bodies of the damned will be incorruptible and immortal, but they will not be glorified like those of the saved (see Matt. 18:8–9). They will then suffer in hell in both soul and body.

St. Paul said that Jesus is the "first fruits" from the dead (1 Cor. 15:20–23). Our Blessed Mother was also assumed body and soul into heaven. Jesus went first, then Mary, and we will follow them at the end of the world.

What will glorified bodies be like? The Gospels record a number of amazing qualities in the body of the resurrected Lord Jesus. He could suddenly appear and then disappear; he passed through walls which implies a power that transcends the principle of physics that two bodies cannot be in the same place at the same time; his body looked the same since the Apostles recognized him, but it was also very different. He could change his appearance so that the two disciples on the road to Emmaus did not recognize him until, at the end of the journey while at table with them "he took the bread and blessed, and broke it, and gave it to them. And their eyes were opened and they recognized him" (Luke 24:13–35).

Catholic tradition holds that the resurrected bodies of the saved will be like the glorified body of Jesus. St. Paul gives us an indication of this: "What is sown is perishable, what is raised is imperishable....It is sown a physical body, it is raised a spiritual body" (1 Cor. 15:42–44).

11   D 801.

Based on the Gospel accounts of the resurrected Christ, theologians have distinguished four special gifts of the risen body of Christ that make it different from our mortal bodies. The resurrected body possesses: 1) *impassibility*, that is, freedom from physical evils of all kinds, such as sickness and death; 2) *subtility*, that is, the spiritualization of the body so that it is completely subject to the soul; 3) *agility*, that is, the ability of the soul to move the body from place to place with ease and rapidity; 4) *clarity*, that is, freedom from all defects and endowment with great beauty and radiance.

The truth about the resurrection of our body on the last day should motivate us to look forward to it with supernatural hope and to motivate us to praise, love and serve God with our whole heart and soul. To godless atheists and secularists, the Catholic belief in the resurrection of the dead is pure myth and utter foolishness. To those of us who believe in Jesus Christ as our God and Savior, who said "I am the resurrection and the life" and proved it by his bodily resurrection on Easter Sunday, his triumph over death is a divine pledge of our own personal resurrection at his Second Coming in glory, if we remain faithful to him and do the will of God.[12]

The General or Last Judgment

According to the revelation of Jesus, the last event in salvation history, before the dawning of the new heaven and the new earth, will be the General or Last Judgment of all human beings created by God from Adam to the last person born. Three mysteries of our faith are closely related and happen more or less simultaneously: the Second Coming of Jesus at the end of the world, the resurrection of the dead and the general judgment. The New Testament is emphatic in stating that there will be a general judgment of all mankind. When world history comes to an end, Christ will come again in glory, accompanied by his angels, as the Eternal Judge of each and every individual person.

---

12   This section is based on *Fundamentals of Catholicism*, Vol. 3, 379–382; see also Ott, *op. cit.*, 488–492.

Belief in the general judgment is an integral part of the Catholic faith. It is included in the articles of faith contained in the Apostles' Creed and in the Nicene Creed which is prayed at the Sunday Mass: "Jesus Christ...ascended into heaven and sits at the right hand of the Father. And he will come again in glory to judge the living and the dead."

In the Gospels Jesus frequently refers to the "day of judgment" or simply "the judgment."[13] He gives the faithful and all those who listen to him plenty of advance warning: "For the Son of Man is to come with his angels in the glory of his Father, and then he will repay every man for what he has done" (Matt. 16:27). The Father has handed over all judgment to the Son and judges the world through Christ: "The Father judges no one, but has given all judgment to the Son, that all may honor the Son, even as they honor the Father....The Father...has given him authority to execute judgment, because he is the Son of man" (John 5:22–27).

St. Peter in the home of Cornelius said that God "commanded us to preach to the people, and to testify that he (Jesus) is the one ordained by God to be judge of the living and the dead" (Acts 10:42). In the Book of Revelation St. John describes the last judgment in terms of rendering an account of all one's deeds which are written down in a book. This seems to be an image or symbol of a spiritual process that takes place all at once (Rev. 20:11–15).

In St. Matthew's Gospel (Matt. 25:31–46) we find a vivid, memorable picture of the Last Judgment in the parable about the sheep and the goats. There the Son of Man, escorted by his angels, takes his seat on the throne of glory. "Before him will be gathered all the nations, and he will separate them one from another as a shepherd separates the sheep from the goats, and he will place the sheep at his right hand, but the goats at the left." (Matt. 25:32–33). The basis of his judgment of salvation or damnation will depend on how generously each person responded to the needs of others during their time on earth because the Lord identifies himself with them: "Truly, I say to you, as you did it to one of the least of these my brethren, you did it to me" (Matt. 25:40).

13 See Matt. 7:22ff.; Ott, *o.p. cit.*, 493.

While the particular judgment deals with individuals and personal morality, the general judgment deals with the social dimension of human existence. So on the last day we will be judged not only as individuals, but also as members of society. This highlights the fact that man is essentially a social being.

An important reason for the General or Last Judgment is that a complete, public and eternally-binding verdict with regard to each person cannot be reached while history is still in progress. Our good deeds and evil deeds have far-reaching effects—have consequences that continue after our death. For example, the goodness of St. Francis of Assisi still motivates many people to imitate him. Archbishop Fulton J. Sheen is still converting men and women to Christ through his many books, CDs and videos on the Internet. Blessed Mother Teresa of Calcutta is a model for many young women who join her Missionaries of Charity in order to take care of the poor. These examples illustrate the fact the final reckoning of the virtue or vice of each person can be made only at the Last Judgment.

Jesus, the Eternal Judge, will evaluate each one of us on the basis of our thoughts, words and deeds. When the Last Judgment will take place no one knows, only the Father. Jesus, of course, in his divine knowledge knew it, but to reveal it to us was not part of the mission he received from his Father. How it will take place is also not known. According to St. Thomas Aquinas, it is probable that the Last Judgment will be in the form of a spiritual enlightenment of all and it will take place in an instant. Because of God's infinite knowledge of all things past, present and future, there will be no need for the courtroom and trials we are familiar with. God will make known immediately, and to all, the merits and the demerits of each person.

Jesus did not reveal where the Last Judgment will take place. The prophet Joel said that the Judgment will take place in "the Valley of Jehoshaphat" which is near Jerusalem (Joel 3:2, 12). According to Ludwig Ott the place is probably to be understood symbolically.[14]

Since it is absolutely certain that each one of us will experience these events and realities: death, particular judgment,

14   *Op. cit.*, 494.

purgatory (probably), heaven or hell, the reuniting of our soul with our body in the resurrection, the Second Coming of Christ in glory, and the Last Judgment—now is the time to secure our salvation and happiness by doing the will of God, keeping the commandments, and daily practicing love of God and neighbor as I prepare myself each day for death and my immediate appearance before the merciful and just Judge who will decide on my eternal future. It is the wise person who provides well in advance for his future. Our Lord has given us sufficient warning about what will happen to us: "He who has ears to hear, let him hear" (Luke 8:8).

CHAPTER 10:
CHRISTIAN BURIAL
OF THE DEAD

Precious in the sight of the Lord is the death of his saints.
(Psalm 116:15)

In the previous chapters our primary concern has been with what happens to the immortal human soul after death when the soul leaves the body. Since man works out his eternal salvation while living on this earth as a soul united to a body, after death the body should be treated with respect because the body was intimately involved in the work of salvation, especially through the reception of the Sacraments of the Church. The body of a Christian has a certain sacredness about it because it received the grace of Christ through Baptism, the Holy Eucharist and the other sacraments. Moreover, Jesus has solemnly promised that, on the last day when he comes in glory to judge the living and the dead, our bodies will rise from the dead to be reunited to our soul forever. Therefore Christians are urged by the Church to treat the bodies of the dead with respect. In order to do that properly the Church has a special liturgy and prayers to be said over the body of the deceased before he or she is buried in the ground. An analysis of that liturgy reveals the thinking of the Church with regard to the condition of the soul of the dead Christian and God's mercy towards him or her.

The burial of a faithful Catholic has a certain relationship to his Baptism. When he was baptized he was brought into the Church being in a state in which his body was alive but his soul was dead in sin. When his corpse is brought into the Church, the body is dead but his soul is alive with the sanctifying grace of Christ. Accordingly, there is a strong sense of hope and joy in the liturgy of Christian burial. The one exception is the Sequence "Dies Irae," used in the extraordinary form of the Roman Rite, which was added to the liturgy in the Middle Ages and stresses fear and dread of the judgment of Christ.

When the body is brought into the church it is placed in the middle of the aisle in front of the altar, with the feet towards the altar if a lay person, but the head towards the altar if a priest. The reason for this is that the lay person walked towards the altar to receive the sacraments, especially the Holy Eucharist; the priest comes from the altar to the people to administer the sacraments.

The positive note of the burial rite is beautifully stated in the Preface of the Mass for the Dead:

> It is truly right and just, our duty and our salvation, always and everywhere to give you thanks, Lord, holy Father, almighty and eternal God, through Christ our Lord. In him the hope of blessed resurrection has dawned, that those saddened by the certainty of dying might be consoled by the promise of immortality to come. Indeed for your faithful, Lord, life is changed not ended, and, when this earthly dwelling turns to dust, an eternal dwelling is made ready for them in heaven.

When the body is placed in the earth it is like planting a seed from which a glorified body will sprout forth on the day of resurrection. When the soul of the faithful Christian leaves the body and appears before the Lord it will either go to heaven immediately or it will be detained for a time to be purified. A human soul separated from the body, however, is incomplete and cannot enjoy complete happiness and perfection until it is reunited to its body. The prayers and ceremonies of the Catholic funeral service cannot be properly understood without faith in purgatory as a state of purification, without faith in the Beatific Vision, without faith in the final resurrection of the body to an incorruptible and immortal life. The blessings of the corpse with holy water and incense, the prayers of the Requiem Mass and the other prayers of absolution and interment at the cemetery are designed to help the deceased person get to heaven as quickly as possible and to bring closure and consolation to the family. This is the communion of saints in action. The Church militant pleads with God for mercy and forgiveness for the soul of the departed.

The Requiem Mass and the prayers of the Church for the repose of the soul of the deceased are proofs from the liturgy of the Church for the existence of purgatory. Why is that so? It is proof because the Church does not pray for those in hell because their status cannot be changed. It is proof because the Church does not pray for the blessed in heaven because they have already attained the final end for which they were created so they do not need our prayers and the prayers will not help them. The Church prays for their intercession with God, but she does not pray *for* them.

For atheists and materialists death is the final end of human existence. For them there is no hope because for them the human person simply ceases to exist at death. Jesus, who is the resurrection and the life, gave us a new view of death. As he said about his friend Lazarus, death is a kind of sleep while we wait for the final resurrection. On this point St. Jerome said: "Death for Christians is not death, but a slumber and a passing sleep."[1]

The high point of the Catholic burial service is the Requiem Mass or the Mass of Resurrection, preferably a High Mass with singing if possible. Through the holy Sacrifice of the Mass the abundant graces of Christ are applied to the soul of the departed Christian. In the funeral Mass the Church commemorates the day of death. The coming of the Lord in the sacrifice, Body, Blood, Soul and Divinity, is related to his coming at the hour of death and also to his coming at the end of the world. The spiritual power of the Mass is so great that as a result the Church sees the departed person as probably already enjoying the Beatific Vision. Accordingly, the procession to the cemetery is presented as a march into Paradise. This idea is expressed in the prayer said at the cemetery or place of committal: "Saints of

1   Quoted in *Roman Ritual* Vol. II, viii; the reference is to 's "Epist. 75 ad Theodor.," PL, XXII, col. 685.

God, come to his/her aid! Hasten to meet him/her, angels of the Lord! May Christ, who called you, take you to himself; may angels lead you to the bosom of Abraham. Eternal rest grant unto him/her, O Lord, and let perpetual light shine upon him/her."[2]

In the Absolution that immediately follows the Requiem Mass special prayers are offered for the deceased that he or she may be delivered from the punishment of sins committed during life. While the priest silently recites the "Our Father" the body is sprinkled with holy water and then incensed. These are outward signs of honor given to the body which was a temple of the Holy Spirit and which one day will rise again in glory endowed with everlasting life. In the extraordinary form of the Roman Rite there is a prayer that makes one think of the last things: "I tremble, and I am sore afraid for the judgment of the wrath to come, when heaven and earth shall be moved. That day is a day of wrath, of woe and tribulation! A great day and exceeding bitter. When Thou shalt come to judge the world by fire....Eternal rest grant unto him (her), O Lord, and let perpetual light shine upon him (her)."[3] The sting of this prayer, however, has been softened by the previous prayer because the person has been elevated by the sacraments of Baptism, Confirmation and Holy Eucharist to be a member of Christ's Mystical Body and so entrusts his soul to God's love and mercy.

The conclusion of the Catholic burial service is the interment or placing the body in the grave. Before the body is lowered the grave is blessed by the priest, if the ground has not already been consecrated, the priest prays: "O God...vouchsafe to bless this grave, and appoint Thy holy angels to keep it; and release the souls of all those whose bodies are buried here from every bond of sin, that they may always rejoice in Thee with Thy saints forever."[4]

2   *Order of Christian Funerals* (New York: Catholic Book Publishing Co. 1998), 126–127.
3   *The Priest's New Pocket Ritual* (New York: The Catholic Book Publishing Co., 1949), 133–134.
4   *Ibid.*

THE MYSTERY OF DEATH AND BEYOND

If at all possible, Catholics should be buried in a Catholic cemetery. The word "cemetery" comes from two Greek words which mean "sleeping place" or "a place for those who are sleeping the sleep of death."[5] The Catholic cemetery is consecrated ground that contains the remains of faithful Catholics who are waiting for the resurrection and the Second Coming of Christ on the last day. It is the temporary resting place of the bodies of those believers who, during their earthly life, were temples of the Holy Spirit and members of the Mystical Body of Christ. The Catholic cemetery with its chapel, Masses, statues of angels and saints is a strong witness to the secular world that we believe in the resurrection of the body and everlasting life.

As the body is lowered into the grave the priest may pray, or a choir sing, if it is present, the "Benedictus" which was prophetically uttered by Zachary, the father of John the Baptist, when his lips were miraculously unsealed (Luke 1:68–79). The prayer praises the coming of the Redeemer and anticipates his final coming in glory at the end of the world. This is a solemn prayer of thanksgiving to God on the part of the Church for our glorious Redeemer and the salvation he has given us. With confidence that the deceased died in Christ in the state of grace and that his or her body will rise gloriously transfigured on the Day of Judgment, the hymn concludes with beautiful words of hope: "I am the resurrection and the life; he that believes in me, though he be dead, shall live; and everyone that lives and believes in me shall not die forever."

5   Nunzio J. Defoe and Joseph H. Doogan, *Why a Catholic Cemetery* (Seattle, WA: Catholic Cemeteries of the Northwest, 1972), 9.

BIBLIOGRAPHY

à Kempis, Thomas, *My Imitation of Christ*. Revised Translation. Brooklyn, NY: Confraternity of the Precious Blood, 1954.

Baker, Kenneth, S.J., *Fundamentals of Catholicism*, Three Volumes. San Francisco: Ignatius Press, 1982.

Catechism of the Catholic Church, Rome: Libreria Editrice Vaticana, 1994.

Catechism of the Council of Trent. Roman Catholic Books, 2002.

Denzinger-Hünermann, *Enchiridion Symbolorum*, 43rd edition. San Francisco: Ignatius Press, 2012.

Flannery, Austin, O.P., *Vatican Council II. The Conciliar and Post Conciliar Documents*. New York: Costello Publishing Co., 1981.

Gabriel of St. Mary Magdalen, O.C.D., *Divine Intimacy*. Rockford, IL: Tan Books and Publishers, Inc., 1996.

Hardon, John A., S.J., *Modern Catholic Dictionary*. New York: Doubleday, 1980.

Lexikon für Theologie und Kirche, Zehnter Band. Frieburg: Verlag Herder 1965.

Neuner, J., S.J.—Dupuis, J., S.J., *The Christian Faith*. New York: Alba House, 1996.

New Catholic Encyclopedia, Volume 4. New York: McGraw-Hill Book Co., 1967.

Nunzio, J. Defoe—Doogan, Joseph H., *Why A Catholic Cemetery*. Seattle, WA: Catholic Cemeteries of the Northwest, 1972.

Order of Christian Funerals. New York: Catholic Book Publishing Co. 1998.

Ott, Ludwig, *Fundamentals of Catholic Dogma*. Rockford, IL: Tan Books and Publishers, Inc., 1974.

Roman Ritual (Ritual Romanum). Available online at www.cantius.org.

The Holy Bible, Revised Standard Version, Catholic Edition. San Francisco: Ignatius
Press, 1994.

The Priest's New Pocket Ritual. New York: The Catholic Book Publishing Co., 1949.